You. Here. Today.

200 Readings for Growth from Codependency to Self-Recovery

Nancy L. Johnston, LPC

YOU. HERE. TODAY.

Published by
Bridge City Books, an imprint of PESI Publishing, Inc.
3839 White Ave
Eau Claire, WI 54703

Cover and interior design by Abby Isackson
Editing by Chelsea Thompson

ISBN 9781962305617 (print)
ISBN 9781962305624 (ePUB)
ISBN 9781962305631 (ePDF)

Printed in Canada.

Dedication

For each of you who are ready to journey within
and connect with your own strength, wisdom, and peace
there for you, here, today.

Contents

Introduction

Daily readings were the foundation of my early recovery from codependency—especially readings from Al-Anon's *One Day at a Time*, the original reader of that twelve-step fellowship for families and friends of people with alcohol use problems.

That was 38 years ago. My husband was just into recovery, and we had a three-month-old daughter. I would get up before anyone else (if I was lucky), get my cup of coffee, and sit and read the meditation for the day as the sun came up. The reading set a helpful tone for my day. It reminded me what I was just starting to learn. It anchored me in my recovery.

I went through that book three times, which means I spent three years, one day at a time, with those readings. It also means I developed a daily practice of connecting to me—what I was feeling, what I needed, what I was working on. It would have been easy to skip the readings and run on to the next thing, but something in me was curious and ready to understand what I could not see about me: What were my relationship anxieties all about? Why was I so afraid of abandonment? How come I had never noticed my efforts to manage and control others? And what was I to do about all of this? I felt insecure in my primary relationship—and at times, outright lost in it—and I wanted something different for me.

A few years into my codependency recovery, I was gifted Melody Beattie's *The Language of Letting Go: Daily Meditations on*

Codependency. This book, too, gave me daily guidance in a new voice that supported my efforts to do as the Al-Anon welcome suggests: keep the focus on my self and not on the alcoholic. That suggestion was eye-opening for me and became what I call my billboard for success. It helped me shift from overfocusing on others to focusing on my needs and the things in my control. Beattie's readings reinforced this healthy focus on self and offered additional understanding, comfort, and direction for my journey. It still does.

In the decades that have gone by, I have learned a lot about codependency, written books about codependency recovery, and more recently have been teaching clinical strategies for working with clients with codependency. I have also continued to work daily on my *self-recovery*, the term I now use for codependency recovery. That, after all, is the heart of codependency recovery: connecting with one's true self.

Recently, I was teaching a group of clinicians about self-recovery, emphasizing the importance of daily practices that help us stay connected with the changes we want to make for ourselves. I mentioned my history with daily readings and was asked about such books to recommend to clients. I mentioned the ones I have written about here and acknowledged that there are more recent ones they might seek out. I was not sure what to recommend.

That's when I realized it: *I want to write my own book of readings!*

I was tired from my long day of teaching and set that idea aside for the night, but the next morning I woke with great enthusiasm for writing this book for you. I have plenty to offer on the topic of codependency recovery that appears in my three other books. It's time to share my learnings in short and sweet ways. It's time to give you a powerful little package to read and carry with you through your day.

This book is a companion to my workbook *The Clinician's Codependency Treatment Workbook: 66 Self-Recovery Strategies for Clients Who Lose Themselves in Others*, with 200 readings distilled from the heart of its lessons. However, this book can also be approached on its own. You don't have to be educated on codependency recovery to benefit from these reflections on the essence of codependency and the elements of self-recovery.

Nor do you have to stick to any schedule or regular rhythm—these readings are not tied to days of the week or seasons of the year. The last thing I wanted was for you to feel bad when you inevitably pick up the book one day and realize it's been a few days (or weeks) since the last time you contemplated a reading. Most of us can relate to feeling guilty for not working our program as we said we would and, perhaps, rushing through all the readings we've missed. But in our haste to catch ourselves up, we end up absorbing less value from the readings than we could. That's why this book is intentionally designed for you to open it anytime, choose one reading for the day, and focus on taking in the meaning it has for you.

The 200 readings are divided into eight sections (listed in the table of contents). The beginning of each section lists the individual readings in that section. You can read the book in the order written, or you can go to the reading that you are drawn to in that moment. If you find that a particular reading invites you to practice something you do not yet understand or feel ready to do, that is fine! You may then find it helpful to turn to the beginning of that section (or even earlier in the book) to focus on developing the awareness and skills that will support you in venturing further into the readings. Whichever way you use the book, I hope you'll spend time with all the readings. They have been crafted as a collection to help you understand where you are, where you may want to grow, and how to grow there.

I said earlier that the foundation of my recovery was established by daily readers. It has been 38 years since I started my recovery journey, and daily readers still help me move forward in that journey. Each day I find an opportunity to practice an idea from these readings or to gain more self-understanding. Each day I reflect on something that deepens my respect and appreciation for my self. Each day I practice sorting my responsibilities from those of others. Each day I grow in my secure relationship-with-myself, learning how to kindly attune and respond to me on a consistent basis as I live with and love others.

I am glad you have joined me in this practice of daily readings for growth from codependency to self-recovery. Self-recovery is a tall order, but it can be met, one reading at a time.

Nancy L. Johnston

Readings on

Understanding Codependency

1

You. Here. Today.

You have made an amazing choice to improve your total health. You have decided to broaden and deepen your connection with your self. You picked up this book today, opened it to this first reading, and are willing to spend a few minutes with *you*. Welcome and congratulations!

No matter what brings you to this book of readings, the important thing is that you are here for you. Something about you probably finds that to be a challenge. You are not alone. Many people focus on others more than on themselves, for lots of reasons.

There is nothing wrong with focusing on others, up to a point. But perhaps you have found that when you neglect your self, you can create problems with your health, relationships, moods, work, or finances.

Perhaps you are here, now, because your balance of self and others is off. That's a great reason to embark on this path of self-recovery and to adopt this book of readings as a traveling companion to help you stay on the new paths you are creating for you.

—

In this moment, let the words of this reading seep in. Allow yourself to acknowledge the importance of focusing on you each day, no matter how short or long that time may be.

2

You are invited to kindly connect with you.

Kindly is the important word here.

You can connect with your self *un*kindly by bringing all sorts of negativity, reprimands, and blame to it. You can spend your precious time telling your self what you should have done, what you did wrong, how you will never learn.

As you move into self-recovery, being kind, open, and compassionate with your self is essential to changing your habitual ways of being with others and self.

Being kind and patient with your self can be challenging at first. It's new territory. So, a good place to start is to become aware of the messages you give your self about you. Are those messages encouraging and supportive, or do they leave you feeling like there is no hope? Do you ask things of your self that you would never ask of a child or a friend? Or are you able to consider your feelings, time, energy, and values and then give your self what you need?

Learning how to kindly connect with your self is what self-recovery is all about.

If you are not yet able to listen and respond to you, no worries. You are in the right place at the right time. Here. Now. Today.

—

In this moment, pay attention to any messages you may be giving your self about you. Just notice. Let your awareness of you step forward.

3

What is codependency?

A person with codependency is dependent on things outside of themselves for their purpose, identity, security, emotional regulation, confidence, and sense of self. They may not be aware of this.

Often, a person with codependency is engaged with another person who is in some way dependent on them to help them with their problems. This is the "co" part of codependency. The other person may have problems with health, addiction, money, housing, work, relationships, sense of self, or personality. This person may not be aware of their dependencies.

Aware or not, the codependent person's involvement with a dependent person intermittently offers the codependent person the security, purpose, and sense of self they seek. This makes for an enmeshed relationship that limits the growth of both people.

Codependency is not necessarily a bad thing. Helping, problem-solving, caring, and protecting others has a lovely place in life. It is human nature to reach out to someone in need or to extend yourself when it is in the best interest for all to do so.

Feeling good about what you have done for others is just fine, up to a point. The problems come when you are too dependent on others for your security and sense of self and have not learned how to be your own source of reassurance and security.

—

In this moment, reflect on this description of codependency. Does any of this sound familiar to you? With kindness and nonjudgment, can you allow yourself to see anything here that may be true for you?

4

A strong external focus keeps you away from you.

External focus is about looking outside of you for what you seek rather than going within your self to find an answer, to feel reassured, or to calm down. We all need things from others, but codependency can leave you too externally focused.

There are good reasons you may have a strong external focus. Your other-centeredness may come from your experiences growing up. Keeping watch outside of your self may have been imperative for your survival. Being hypervigilant or scanning your environment in order to read situations was necessary and helpful. You may have received messages that no one wanted to hear from you, that you should simply do as you were told.

Your external focus was adaptive and protective, but it kept you from being able to also tune into you. In the process of paying attention to others, you disconnected from your own thoughts, emotions, and needs. It was not safe or helpful for you to attend to them.

Life requires that you have some external focus. You are in relationship with others constantly, *and* you want to be able to connect with your self as well. Self-recovery is all about helping you develop your internal focus that has been waiting for you all along.

—

In this moment, without judging your self, consider your external focus. Are you aware when you look to others for reassurance? Is your emotional condition dependent on how someone else is? Watch for your external focus as you go through your day.

5

Self-sacrificing has its limits.

Doing things for others is human nature. Caring about and wanting to help others can be good for all. The other person benefits, and you feel connected and valued.

The problems come when your sense of self is dependent on this giving of self to others. If you are not considering your self even as you are offering your self to others, you can be depleting or denying your self what it needs.

Sacrificing means giving up something important to you. That could range from giving money you really don't have to letting go of planned time alone. Sometimes you do have to sacrifice; it's what will best serve the situation you're in. Sometimes, though, no one is asking you to sacrifice. Without awareness, you may be operating out of your people-pleasing, "How can I help?" modes.

Self-sacrifice has its costs. Slowly but surely, your health, energy, and good spirit waste away. You may feel angry with others, unfairly treated, or disrespected. You may feel jealous of people who seem to have time for themselves and who do what they want to do. Most of all, you wonder why people don't care for you as you care for them.

Learning how to consider your self as you consider the needs of others can keep you from falling into this unhappy imbalance.

In this moment, notice what emotions have come up for you as you read about self-sacrifice. Whatever they are, your emotions are messages to you from you and will be helped by your noticing and spending time with them.

6

Is problem-solving a specialty of yours?

If you are good at solving problems, congratulations! That is a great ability to have.

People with codependency often are good problem-solvers. That's what we do. From getting your stalled car to the mechanic to helping your child complete their homework before bedtime, you see the problem and instinctively jump in with a solution . . . sometimes even when not requested.

And that's where your problem-solving can be problematic.

Pushing your excellent problem-solving skills onto others can itself be a problem for them and for you. The other person may not see the problem as you see it. They may not want to resolve the problem, or just not in the way you think is best. They may feel crowded or disempowered by your offers to problem-solve for them.

Meanwhile, you may feel hurt that your ideas (which were not solicited) are not well received. You may be tired from the work you have invested in trying to solve the problem. You may be worried about what will happen if the problem is not resolved.

If the problem is not yours, turn your focus back to your own problems. If the unsolved problem does or will affect you, you will learn lots more in other readings about assertiveness and setting healthy boundaries to help you with that more complex situation. Until then, use your problem-solving talents to help you with your own challenges and opportunities.

—

In this moment, kindly consider whether your ability to problem-solve can go too far. Do you jump in with ideas and solutions ahead of others? Do you spend mental time problem-solving a situation that is not yours?

7

Maybe you identify as "a fixer."

"I am a fixer" has been declared by many a codependent person. They mean it as a defining aspect of who they are, like saying "I am a parent" or "a teacher" or "a chef." They mean that being a fixer is a way they operate in the world, consciously and unconsciously.

Being a fixer is handy. Who doesn't want something fixed when it is broken? But fixing can go too far. It has a place and purpose if it is desired, requested, or lifesaving, and if it is consciously offered. It becomes a problem when you lose your self in fixing—that is, when your fixing-self is unconsciously driving your day.

If you spend too much time figuring out how to fix something or someone, get too attached to things being fixed, or independently take action to fix something without including the other people involved, your relationships with others suffer damage and your connection with your self begins to disappear.

—

In this moment, consider whether you identify as a fixer. Fixing can serve you well, and it can also become too much for you and others. Spend some time with your fixer part and hear what it has to say to you.

8

Expressing your emotions may not be your thing.

For a number of possible reasons, you may not be good at expressing your emotions. Perhaps no one wanted to hear about your emotions when you were growing up, or perhaps you are afraid your feelings will overtake you if you allow them to come forward. Or perhaps you are just not aware of your emotions as they arise.

Having emotions is part of your humanness. You cannot avoid them or deny them. They naturally occur as you live your life. It is normal to feel disappointed, confused, nervous, attracted to someone or something. Your emotions are real responses to what happens in your life or to things you are thinking. You cannot control emotions or make them go away.

You *can* learn to offer yourself emotional care.

Stuffing your emotions has been identified as a core feature of codependency. That makes sense. Whether you are denying your honest emotions or trying to ignore them, you are disconnecting from a very important part of who you are. This disconnection keeps you from acknowledging your whole self. Your body, mind, and spirit are all affected by your emotions. Their interconnection is profound and radiates through your whole being.

When you are ready to notice, allow, and care for your emotions, your whole self will be glad.

—

In this moment, notice what emotions may have come up for you as you read this reading about expressing emotions. Just notice, as you are ready.

9

More on the "co" in codependency.

"Co" means jointly or mutually. You are familiar with such words as *co-chairperson* or *co-teachers*. Co's work together to a particular end.

We've talked about how a person with codependency is dependent on others for their sense of self, value, or emotional care. Often, the important other person they are engaged with is dependent on them for something in turn.

The other person may depend on the codependent person for help with their health, finances, mood, behaviors, housing, sense of purpose, or structuring their life. Some of this dependency may be because of their health or developmental needs. Some of it may be addiction-related. Some of it may be the result of relationship entanglements that foster enmeshment.

The dependency of the other person gives the codependent person the sense of purpose and value they seek, but this sense can be too reliant on what this other person says or does. In this case, both people are mutually fostering each other's dependencies.

Sometimes this mutual dependency isn't obvious, even when we feel it. That may be why you are reading this book. It's likely that something has seemed wrong in your important relationships, and you could not put your finger on it. Noticing the interplay between you and others in this dimension of codependency can help you see more clearly the ties that bind you.

—

In this moment, consider an important someone in your life. Are you aware of what you depend on them for? Are you aware of what they depend on you for? How do you feel about those dependencies?

10

Perhaps you never thought of yourself as dependent.

You may be a strong, independent person. You may take care of an amazing number of things in a day. People can count on you to get things done. You are attentive and reliable. So how in the world could you be "dependent"?

It's likely that your dependencies are hidden from you behind the high level of competence you bring to your interactions. As you help, fix, problem-solve, or manage things in the lives of people who are important to you, you lose awareness of your motivation for doing all these things.

When you are competent, you enjoy what you are able to accomplish, so you do more. When you are on autopilot, you do more. When your habitual patterns of caretaking and productivity keep things running smoothly, you do more.

And as you do more, your motivations for what you are doing get further and further from your awareness, until one day . . . you explode!

This may have happened to you. Perhaps you were being your responsible self, juggling the people, places, and things of your day, and your internal system short-circuited. You got upset, felt unappreciated, quit, threw something, or fell into tears. Your internal system went haywire—that system you are starting to tune into instead of being stuck on external focus all the time.

—

In this moment, consider whether you have ever overloaded yourself without being aware of how much you were taking on and why.

11

You may ask yourself, "What am I dependent on others for?"

As you are ready, tune into your internal channel with kindness and curiosity and see what dependencies may lie within you. What do you seek through your caregiving, problem-solving, fixing, and managing of others?

As you look, try to offer yourself compassion rather than judgment. Dependencies are not necessarily bad. But they can also be a problem when you cannot give yourself what you seek.

So, what might you be dependent on others for? Here's a quick list to help you get your thinking going: approval, confidence, self-esteem, belonging, purpose, value, reassurance, commitment.

You might depend on others to regulate your emotions: *I'm okay if everyone else is okay.*

You might depend on others to make decisions about things in your personal life: *Should I buy this? How do I look in this outfit? What would you do?*

You might depend on others to be as helpful and considerate of you as you are to them: *If I do this for them, surely they will do the same for me.*

Within a moderate range, interdependencies have a place in healthy relationships. But when you are not aware of them, dependencies can lock you into codependent patterns of seeking in others what you want to be able to give to your self.

—

In this moment, consider how you feel about this idea that you may have some dependencies of your own embedded in all you do. What might they be?

12

Being too focused on others can cause you problems.

Have you ever been driving a car and were so focused on a conversation you were having that you missed your exit? Have you ever gone grocery shopping and got so interested in a new product that you forgot to buy what you went into the store for?

This type of distracted focus can happen in relationships, too. You can have your schedule for your day pretty much set and ready to go, and your child gets sick. You can have plans for a nice evening with friends, and your partner remembers they've promised their parents you'll have dinner with them.

On a more serious note, you may be in a relationship where your safety requires that you keep a steady focus on the other person. You may be in a relationship where the other person's health issues demand your attention and care. You may be in a relationship with someone you fear will abandon you, so you vigilantly watch them.

Realistically, life *will* draw you away from your plans and connection with self at times. For helpful and protective reasons, you will focus on others. When this happens, remember to keep an eye on your own ball, too. Otherwise, you may miss your exit, forget what you went to the store for, or lose track of who you are and what you are wanting for you and your life. That would be a problem.

—

In this moment, consider whether your focus on others is causing problems for you. Have you missed any exits recently that were important to you?

13

There are a number of behaviors associated with codependency.

It can be helpful to think of codependency in terms of its associated behaviors. When we look at specific behaviors, we can see more clearly how we may have become lost in someone else.

Behaviors associated with codependency include giving, fixing, caregiving, helping, problem-solving, people-pleasing, conflict avoiding, taking over, and controlling. To a certain degree, these behaviors are not problematic. They are normal human actions that often come from care, concern, and compassion. It is when you carry these behaviors too far that they cause problems for you and others.

Different people engage in different behaviors associated with codependency. Some are fixers. Some are overly caregiving. Some speak for others or do for others what that other person could do for themselves. Some people need to be in control of most things.

You do not have to do all of these behaviors associated with codependency to be a codependent person. You likely have your own natural or learned ways you extend yourself for others.

—

In this moment, think about which behaviors associated with codependency you engage in. Maybe you have never thought about codependency in this much detail before. Take time to look again at the list of behaviors in this reading. Are any true for you? Do you extend yourself to others in additional ways not listed above?

14

Think of your behaviors associated with codependency on a continuum.

It is helpful to think of codependent behaviors on a continuum from okay to too far. You want to offer kindnesses to others, and it is important to notice when you are offering too much, too often, or more than you have to give.

Considering codependent behaviors on a continuum reinforces the fact that helping, serving, or even doing things to please others is not bad in and of itself. As we all live together, it is important that we know how to consider others, compromise, give, and sometimes self-sacrifice.

But if self-sacrificing and self-abandonment are your predominant ways of being in relationship with others, there is bound to be a personal cost to you. Self-neglect may have been a protective way of being for you sometime in your life, but in the long run, not knowing how you feel or not having a safe place to be who you are is damaging to your body, mind, emotions, and spirit.

Self-recovery involves learning to notice not only your codependent behaviors but also where they fall on the continuum from okay to too far. If you find they are going too far and causing you problems, you will learn how to adjust yourself along the continuum back into the okay range where, hopefully, you will feel some peace within.

—

In this moment, picture the continuum in your mind.
See "okay" on the left end and "too far" on the right end.
Now, think of a codependent behavior you are currently engaged in and find its range on this continuum.
For now, that's all you need to seek: simple awareness.

15

Staying within the okay range of codependent behaviors is healthy for all.

As you think about codependent behaviors on a continuum, from okay to too far, you may wonder what the okay range looks like. How would you know if you are operating in that zone?

Let's say you are wanting to cook and deliver a meal to a friend who recently had surgery. You offer to do this for them, but they say, "No thanks. Not right now." They already have plenty of meals in the fridge.

When you are caregiving in the okay range, you are able to make an offer and accept the other person's yes or no. In this case, you respect their "no thanks" and don't take a meal to them. You may feel disappointed or rejected by their response, but you are able to remind yourself that they have their own feelings and needs, and stop yourself from doing it anyway in favor of honoring what the other person has said they want.

In the okay range, you are able to be flexible and open with how things unfold. You do your part and respect what others bring to the table. You stay connected with your feelings and impulses and take responsibility for them so as not to tread on the other person. This keeps your relationships with others and with yourself in good order. No one feels run over, and perhaps you have a bit more space for you.

—

In this moment, can you imagine what it might feel like to operate in the okay range of behaviors associated with codependency? Does staying in this range appeal to you? What might challenge your ability to stay in this okay range?

16

Your efforts to help, fix, or manage can go too far.

Have you ever tried to help someone and realized you had carried it too far? Maybe they got mad at you for your efforts. Maybe you became resentful for all you were doing for them. Maybe they did not seem grateful or willing to receive what you were offering. You became entangled with them.

And you were just trying to help.

This is where codependency can be a problem—when, without awareness, you have taken back the ball when it was in someone else's court. When you do this, you lose your connection with *you* as you become increasingly involved with the other person.

It's your loss of your connection with your self that then causes you problems. You are no longer in touch with your needs, feelings, desires, and values. You are overfocused on the other person's needs, feelings, desires, and values. Your ability to consider your self has greatly diminished or disappeared.

Moreover, you are likely to run into relationship problems with the other person who is not appreciating your enthusiasm or whom you may now feel is taking advantage of you.

—

In this moment, can you identify a codependent behavior of yours that you tend to carry too far? How do you know you are going too far? What within you tells you this important information?

17

Addiction lives at the very far end of the continuum of codependent behaviors.

Codependency can become an addiction.

A person with an addiction is not able to control their use of a substance or their engagement in particular behaviors. They may want to limit their use or behaviors. They may want to not use or engage in those behaviors at all. But their efforts to limit themselves are very difficult for them to enforce. Obsessive thoughts and compulsive behaviors are other ways to describe addiction.

When any of the behaviors associated with codependency travel to the "too far" end of the continuum, addiction is likely present. At that end, the person with codependency cannot stop themselves from trying to fix, care for, or manage the other person, despite the negative consequences that may be coming from their obsessiveness. Loss of control and continued use or engagement despite negative consequences are both signs of addiction.

Pay attention to where you are on the continuum of codependent behaviors. Notice if you are traveling into the more complicated zone of addiction. Noticing and being able to stop yourself early on is a reliable way to not let your codependency run away with you.

The word "addiction" is strong and often unwelcome. How do you feel about even the possibility that codependency can be an addiction? Are you able to recognize when your codependent behaviors are dangerously close to the obsessive/compulsive/addictive zone?

18

Careful: You can overfunction for others.

Overfunctioning for others can be a helpful way to understand codependency.

As you are already learning, codependency is about going too far in what you offer to others, how preoccupied you are in your thoughts about someone else, or how compulsive your codependent behaviors are. You just can't stop your self.

"Over" is the important part of overfunctioning. You can over-do, over-explain, over-defend, over-protect, over-deny, or over-compensate for someone else. You can take more than your share of responsibility or keep shifting your boundaries to accommodate the other person.

"Over" is about carrying your codependent behaviors too far—doing for the other person what they can do for themselves, avoiding conflict by denying your own self, pleasing others without awareness of what would please you.

Overfunctioning can come from a good place within you, but it can interfere with the healthy growth of each person in your relationships, including and especially you.

—

In this moment, think about this idea of overfunctioning for others. Do you relate to this idea? Is it helpful as a way of noticing how focused you may be outside of your self?

19

Careful: You can underfunction in your own life.

Underfunctioning in your own life is the other side of the same coin as overfunctioning for others.

If you are busy taking care of others, it is almost impossible to take good care of you, too. Have you ever stayed up late to help someone with their deadline and missed out on your sleep? Have you given more money than you could really afford to someone you felt was in need? Have you covered for someone's mistakes when they were clearly responsible for those mistakes? Have you helped others keep their appointments while failing to schedule your own?

When you underfunction in your life, you neglect care for your own health and wellness. As you regularly neglect your own care, you may develop problems with your body, or your moods, or your relationships with friends and family.

When you underfunction in your life, you fail to consider your self in plans and decisions made at work, at home, and in friendships. You don't think about what you want or what might work for you. You do not represent your self when others make decisions that affect you. You do not put yourself into the formula of the life you are living.

Persistent underfunctioning in your life can have you lying for others, going bankrupt for them, or generally operating in ways that are not true to your values and beliefs.

—

In this moment, think about how far you go in underfunctioning in your own life. Are you feeling any consequences from neglecting your self as you overfunction for others?

20

Your kind gestures and considerateness mean no harm.

The tricky thing about overfunctioning for others is that it often starts from a good place within you. A desire to help, an idea for solving a problem, saving the other person the trouble of having to do something—all can be legitimate reasons for extending your self to someone else. It's your thoughtful humanness in action.

But when overextending your self for others becomes a habitual pattern or causes you to underfunction in your own life, that's when problems occur in your health and relationships.

Even more foundationally, when you overfunction for others and underfunction for you, you are inadvertently keeping each of you from your own healthy growth.

When you do for others what they can do for themselves, they won't learn how to do it. When you cover for them, they won't learn to take responsibility for themselves. When you step in too quickly and don't give the other person space to act on their own behalf, they believe you see them as incapable.

When you overextend your self for others, you are not able to also attend to your thoughts, feelings, and behaviors and make conscious decisions that are for your own good. This self-disregard conveys the message to you that what you need and want is not as important as what others need and want. Needless to say, that message does not foster your growing sense of self.

—

In this moment, see if you can open your self to this idea that overdoing for others limits the growth of each of you.

21

If you are too focused on someone else, you lose your connection with you.

Multitasking is a real thing. You probably do it a number of times over the course of the day. While you are cooking dinner, you're preparing lunches for tomorrow. While you are walking, you return phone calls. While you are driving, you eat.

Over the decades, there has been debate about whether multitasking is any more effective than doing one thing at a time. This reading is not about resolving that question. This reading is to acknowledge that when you are doing more than one thing at a time, you are not able to pay full attention to any one thing. Your mind is skipping around all the time.

This is true in your relationships as well. Relationships can be like multitasking. Depending on how many characters are in your story at any moment, each is likely asking you for some kind of attention. As you pay attention to others in your life, your connection with your self is disrupted. It almost has to be at times. But remember: Your self-connection is a valuable internal channel, full of important information for you, as a radio channel might be. If you're living with an interrupted internal connection most or all of the time, you may forget that you have that channel or completely lose the service to it.

Your internal connection is your foundation to your good health. It is where your body, mind, emotions, and spirit are all telling you valuable things to consider as you make decisions, take action, respond to others, and act on your own behalf.

—

In this moment, see if you can stop multitasking for five minutes—whether that is with actual tasks or with people—and tune into your own internal channel.

22

You can actually lose yourself in someone else.

Have you ever lost your self in a book, a movie, an art project, a workout? You lost track of time and whatever else you had planned to do. In some ways, it was great to take a break from it all. Getting lost can feel refreshing.

In other ways, there may have been uncomfortable consequences: you missed an appointment; you had to rush to get where you were supposed to be; it was too late to prepare for the next day. Coming back to your reality was abrupt and demanding, and it likely required reorienting your self.

You can lose your self in a relationship, too. Perhaps you are reading this book because you know this already—you *have* lost your self in someone else. Either the other person is very demanding of your time and attention, or you are obsessed with them and can't focus on anything else. (Or both.)

As you spend increasing time thinking about, worrying about, or doing things for or with someone else, your connection with you diminishes. As that happens, you may feel increasingly lost as to what to say and do in that relationship or for your self.

It's like being on a hike in the woods where you have been relying on blazes on the trees to tell you where the trail is. All of a sudden, you are not seeing the blazes and have not been paying any attention to the direction you have actually been traveling in. You have not noticed landmarks or the position of the sun to orient you. You don't know where you are. You are lost.

—

In this moment, take in this image of
losing your way on a hike in the woods.
Have you ever felt like this in your relationships?

23

Being lost does not feel good.

Being lost does not feel good at all.

Being lost in the woods, on the highway, or even while trying to find the location of a new coffee shop can be very frustrating. You don't know which way to turn. You go one way and then another and get increasingly irritated and agitated if you are not finding your way.

Sometimes you also feel scared when you are lost. Fear is a deep, real emotion. You may feel scared that you will never find your way and something bad will happen to you. Your survival instincts of fight, flight, or freeze may kick in. These reactions can help you survive, but they likely won't help you find your way. They interfere with your ability to think clearly and rationally.

Any and all of these emotions can arise when you have lost your self in someone else. The strongest and most upsetting feelings come when you actually realize you are lost in your relationship and don't know what to do! Perhaps the other person has been your compass, and all of a sudden you don't like the direction they are taking you or you don't even know where you are headed.

Having and using your own internal compass can help a lot in these moments of being lost. Better yet, it can help you to not get lost in the first place. These readings are intended to support you in developing your internal compass, a guide you can always rely on.

—

In this moment, imagine having an internal compass that you can trust.

24

An enmeshed relationship can eclipse both you and the person you are in relationship with.

Here's a way to think about relationships. Each person in the relationship is represented by a circle-of-self. The circumference of the circle represents the boundaries of each person—that is, their ownership of their individual thoughts, feelings, needs, and wants.

In an enmeshed relationship, the circles-of-self of the two individuals overlap, mostly or even completely, and are often stuck in this pattern. Occasionally, this type of enmeshment works for people, but more often, enmeshment keeps each person from developing and honoring their own self. Instead, each person in this enmeshed relationship defines self through the other person and may not have healthy autonomy over their own thoughts and behaviors.

This overlap of the circles-of-self is like an eclipse. As the circles remain over each other, each person is being eclipsed by the other person. There may only be a sliver of self on the edge of the overlapped circles. Think about viewing a solar eclipse. You watch with anticipation as the moon crosses the sun. You notice the dark that comes with this intersection and the chill in the air that results. Imagine that the crossing stops once the sun is blocked by the moon and that you are stuck in a dark, cold environment.

It's hard to grow when it's dark and cold.

—

In this moment, think about this idea of enmeshment in a relationship: being eclipsed intentionally or unintentionally by someone else or by your own fears and insecurities. Have you had this experience?

ENMESHED

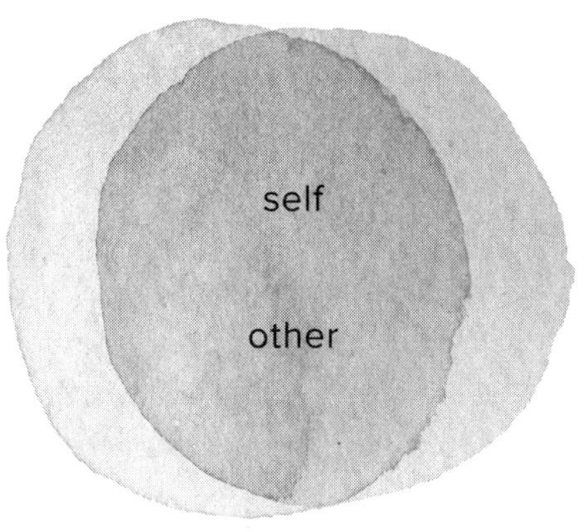

25

An alienated relationship can keep you from being true to yourself.

Let's play further with the idea of circles-of-self.

Whereas an enmeshed relationship is where two people in the relationship eclipse each other, an alienated relationship is where two individuals hardly intersect at all. They may be in the same household, family system, or workplace, but they say as little as possible to each other or prefer to avoid each other.

These may be necessary coping mechanisms, or they may not be. Such alienation can start from an unresolved disagreement and become habitual. It's easier to just not say anything, to give the cold shoulder, or to roll your eyes and walk away.

Relationship alienation is about not being true to your self. As you are avoiding interaction with the other person, you are having to deny or squelch your thoughts and feelings. Again, perhaps this is self-protective, but it can also be blocking you from an improved relationship with this person. You may be so mad that you worry you will lose control if you say anything to them. You may want to avoid conflict or fear not pleasing them. You may even worry they will leave you if you speak your truth.

So, you remain alienated, orbiting each other on a regular basis but with no honesty or intimacy. Intimacy comes from being able to be who you are as you are safely in relationship with them.

—

In this moment, let's say, "Who hasn't rolled their eyes and walked away sometimes?" The deeper question is, who were you walking away from: them or your self or both?

25

ALIENATED

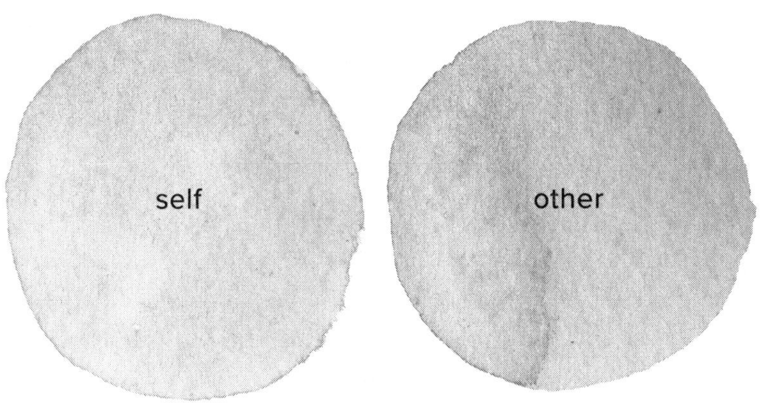

26

Healthy relationships are dynamic, alternating back and forth from close to individuated.

Once again, let's bring the relationship circles into mind. Remember, each circle represents an individual—their thoughts, emotions, hopes, wishes, dreams, and values, to name just a few of the dimensions within each of us.

It's helpful to stop and simply recognize how different each of us is, with multiple parts of self that make us unique. This alone is an important awareness that can help you with recovery from codependency. A person with codependency can forget this and impose their own thoughts, feelings, or values on someone else. This is how we end up believing we know what is best for a person who is different from us.

In a healthy relationship, the circles-of-self can move toward or away from each other flexibly. They can be entirely separate at times. They can overlap to various degrees, offering shared experiences in their relationship and simultaneous healthy connections with self. This dynamic flow of closeness and individuation between these two people acknowledges individual differences and is founded on mutual trust and respect.

You would probably love to be in a healthy relationship. Most of us desire that, and most of us weren't taught how to make that dream come true. You can't necessarily control what someone else brings to the relationship, but you can learn more about what you can bring that promotes this healthy, respectful flow. Cultivating your connections with you is a great start!

—

In this moment, think of an important relationship you are currently in. Does it have a together/separate flow that is based on mutual trust and respect?

HEALTHY

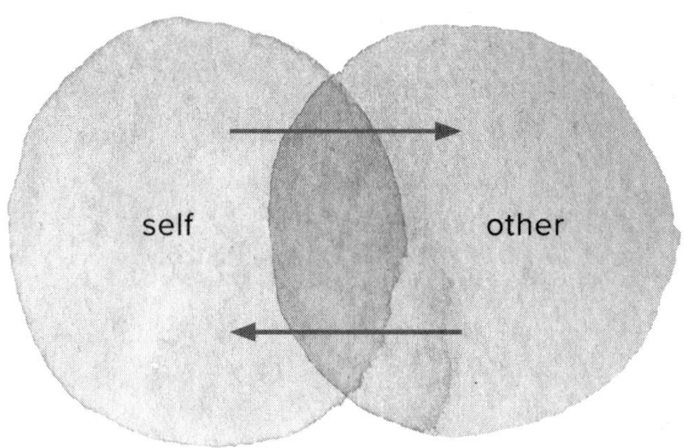

27

Imagine being in a relationship with mutual respect.

Respect means that you recognize and honor who the other person is—what they believe, how they spend their time, the choices they make for themselves. Doing this involves acknowledging their uniqueness and the ways they are different from you. It does not mean you agree with them on all fronts, but you hear and see them for who they are and choose to be in a relationship with them.

Mutual respect goes both ways. Both individuals offer each other space and respect for who the other person is. They may express their disagreements, offer different points of view, or sometimes compromise with each other, but this communication is all done in the context of honoring the differences between them.

How are you with respecting the differences of you and others? Codependency can be tricky. You believe you are trying to help or make things better for someone else. To some degree, this is likely true, but you can also be doing these things because you believe you know what is best for someone else and are inadvertently imposing that message on them. As you do this, it is likely that the other person either moves away from you or pushes back against you. A relationship entanglement ensues. Neither of you feels respected by the other.

Mutual respect feels good. You have the safe space to be true to you, and the other person has the same for themselves.

—

In this moment, consider what mutual respect really means and entails.

28

As you learn to respect your self, you more readily require respect from others.

You can probably think of people whom you respect. They may be in your home, at work, among your friends, or in the broader world. You know what respecting someone feels like. You want to hear what they have to say; you believe they know what they are talking about; you think they have good ideas; you appreciate how they do things.

Self-recovery is about learning to respect your self in these same ways—being able to listen, believe in, honor, and appreciate you. Do you ever think of your self in these respectful ways? If you have grown up disconnected from you, or if recent life circumstances have drawn you away from you, you may have trouble trusting your own judgment and actions. Self-respect may be something you hardly ever experience.

It takes time to learn to trust and respect your self. First, you make the valuable shift from being too focused on others to tuning into your thoughts, feelings, wants, needs, and values. Next, you learn skills that help you think more clearly and take actions consistent with what you have come to know is true for you.

Over even more time, as you speak and act on your own behalf, you will come to trust your judgment and know the feelings of internal safety and security that come from the respect you have developed for you. And as you develop this respect for your self, you will more readily require respect from others as well—nothing less.

—

In this moment, think of something you have said or done this week that you respect your self for.

29

In a healthy relationship, you don't have to hold on for dear life.

"Holding on for dear life"—that's an expression you have probably heard. It is a meaningful way to describe the desperation and energy being put into a situation in which one fears the potential loss of something very important.

Having to hold on for dear life in a relationship is not desirable. Riding the waves of moods, upsets, unpredictability, unknowns, or betrayals is not good for either person in the relationship.

For you, a person wanting to grow from codependency into self-recovery, this reading is a loving reminder that in a healthy relationship you can trust and respect each other. You are not responsible for each other. You can support and encourage each other, but each of you has your own responsibilities to take care of—physical, emotional, and practical.

A healthy relationship means being equal partners. You cannot make someone else be your equal partner, but you can learn how to be one to them. You can do your part and step back so the other person can do their part. You can support them as you also support your own life.

Pulling and tugging is a fight. Holding on tightly only creates more stress and imbalance. Learning to simultaneously be with the other person and with your self—respecting differences and appreciating what you share—can help you release your grip and quiet your relationship fears.

—

In this moment, consider whether you may be holding on to something or someone too tightly, trying to make things work and fearing what may happen if you don't.

30

The health of a relationship depends on the health of each person in the relationship.

A relationship cannot be healthier than the health of each person in that relationship.

If you are cooking and one of your ingredients has gone bad, the dish you are preparing does not turn out right. If one of the spark plugs in your car is not firing, the car doesn't run well. And so it is with a relationship.

If one person in the relationship has to take on more to sustain the relationship, both individuals will ultimately feel the unhealthy consequences of that imbalance. If one person has to lean on the other, the person being leaned on will wear out and collapse in some way, and the other person—who is no longer supported by the other—will fall.

Each person needs to be doing their personal work to understand their relationship patterns, heal their old wounds, and take responsibility for themselves. It is not the responsibility of one person in the relationship to fix the other.

In a healthy relationship, the individuals do their own work and support the efforts each is making toward their own wellness.

Clearly, you are working on your self. You are spending time with these readings and learning new things about you and relationships. You are here for you. Great job! Read on. You and all of your relationships will benefit from your self-recovery.

—

In this moment, appreciate your openness to understanding your self and learning how to keep a kind connection with you as you are in relationship with others.

Readings on

Understanding Self-Recovery

31

Good care of you is not selfish.

You can grow from codependency into self-recovery. You can become better at stopping and checking in with you and at knowing how to respond to all that you find within you. The readings in the remainder of this book will fill you with ideas and inspiration for your self-recovery.

If you are not clear on what self-recovery means or how to do that, that's okay. Reading by reading, you will be taking in new thoughts as well as invitations to be more balanced in your relationships with others and with your self.

An important place to start is the knowledge that taking good care of you is not selfish.

People working on their codependency often say, "I would do X for my self, but wouldn't that be selfish?" The notion of speaking up for your self or of taking time for your self can be foreign. If you are usually attending to others, turning your attention within can feel odd and indulgent. Guilt may well show up.

Believe it or not, taking good care of your self not only improves your health and well-being but can also improve the relationships you are concerned about. If you are rested, you have more energy and your outlook improves. If you have done what you wanted to do for you today, you feel centered and accomplished. If you speak up for you, you feel noticed, heard, and connected with your sense of self.

—

In this moment, consider that taking care of your self creates a solid foundation for your health and the health of your relationships. It is not selfish. Everyone benefits, especially you.

32

You have lots of internal goings-on that no one else knows about.

As you are learning, self-recovery is about tuning into you. That's your internal world. People and situations outside of you are your external worlds. Paying attention to both is the balance you seek in self-recovery.

As you learn to shift your focus to your internal world, you may be surprised at all the goings-on in there. On the outside, you may appear put-together and on your game. People think you do so much for so many, so well. They say they don't know how you do it.

Truth be told, you also wonder how you do it all. How do you pull off a day full of tasks on behalf of others? How do you put up with problems unfairly left for you to take care of? How do you not fall apart in some way—into tears or an outburst? Why do you keep adding to your lists without checking in with you first?

As you pause and listen to you, don't be surprised to find that you have strong feelings, thoughts, and impulses waiting to be noticed by you and for you. These are important messages that you can learn to listen to and grow from. No one else needs to know about these goings-on right now. They are there to communicate with you about you as you begin to develop your relationship-with-self.

—

In this moment, notice if you have any awareness of what's going on within you. Do you have moments of being tuned into your thoughts, feelings, body, or spirit? If so, do you move toward or away from your awareness?

33

Anxiety and depression can spring from your codependent ways.

Anxiety and depression are two common mental health issues that can range from mild to problematic. They can show up separately or together.

Anxiety is about worrying unnecessarily about any number of things. It can include being fearful, feeling nervous, or expecting the worst.

Depression is related to a sad mood. It can show itself through problems with sleep, appetite, energy, and outlook on life.

You may be familiar with one or both of these issues. You may have sought help for anxiety or depression. That's a good step to take.

What you may not be aware of is that anxiety and depression can spring from your codependent ways. Codependency can be an underlying way of being that is contributing to your emotional condition.

With codependency, you are so focused on others that you may neglect your anxiety or depression. Your focus on others may have you feeling extra anxious about what may happen to them or depressed because you have not been able to fix or change them.

These are normal feelings up to a point, but if you are preoccupied with the other person—if your efforts to help, fix, or manage have gone too far—anxiety and depression can arise as you fail to get the results you are hoping for from the other person.

—

In this moment, consider if you are experiencing anxiety, depression, or perhaps both. Then go a bit deeper and wonder if your focus on others may be contributing to those emotions.

34

Let's bring a no blame, shame, or judgment energy to self-recovery work.

Bringing no blame, shame, or judgment to your self-recovery work is essential to connecting with your self and fostering your own growth.

Imagine trying to raise a child or a pet in a harsh and negative environment. It is almost too upsetting to think about, let alone experience. You certainly don't want to do this to your self, either, as you learn to attune and respond to you.

You may have received shame or judgment from your family as you grew up or from someone you are currently in a relationship with. It is all too easy to adopt those voices and hear them in your head, telling you what a hopeless mess you are. Such messages keep your codependent patterns repeating. They lead you to believe that if you can ever say or do the right thing for someone else, you will finally be an okay person.

Rather than judging yourself for how you feel or what you have done, self-recovery is about learning to notice feelings and actions without negativity toward self. Yes, you have made choices you regret, but you are not stupid. Yes, you just did the thing you said you were not going to do again, but that doesn't mean you can't make the changes you want for you.

You will inevitably judge your self sometimes. When that happens, don't judge your self for your judging. Instead, notice your judgment, notice what you are saying to your self about you, and see if you can speak a bit more kindly to you.

—

In this moment, can you think of a compassionate statement you can say to your self when you notice you are blaming, shaming, or judging your self?

35

Being dependent on others for your sense of self is fragile.

Being dependent on others for your sense of self means looking to others to know how you should feel, think, or act. You watch for approval and disapproval. You mold your self to accommodate the feedback you are getting so that you please others, avoid conflict, or take care of the emotions of someone else while you minimize your own.

Sure, your sense of self is based in part on your relationships, but having your sense of self be fully dependent on what you are getting from other people in your life is fragile. The messages you get from them may be inconsistent and confusing. The accommodating you are willing to do may not truly suit your nature.

Sometimes you will simply not know what they think of you or wish you would do. You will have no outside data from which to know how you are or what to do. To complicate things, you may pursue that information from the other person, driving them away and leaving you feeling further lost inside.

Self-recovery is about building your sense of self from the inside out. It is about knowing what you think and feel on your own. It is about knowing your values and living into those values. It is about becoming consistent in what you say and do. It is about listening to others and then arriving at what is true for you.

—

In this moment, consider if your sense of self is more dependent on others than you wish. Does your sense of self feel fragile at times? Might your sense of self feel more solid if it were based within you?

36

You are learning to stop and ask yourself, "What do I want for me?"

To shift your focus to your internal world, the first step is to stop your self when you are about to fall into your usual patterns of focusing on the needs and wants of others to the exclusion of your own. Stopping creates space for checking in with self.

Stopping your self literally means a full stop, the way we do when we are driving and come upon a red light. While you are waiting for the traffic to clear (that is, the "traffic" in your mind or heart), ask your self, "What do I want for me?"

This is not a selfish question. It is simply an honest noticing of what is going on with you. It is only fair that as you consider the needs, wants, and feelings of the other person you also consider yours. Fair. Mutual. Respectful.

It may take longer than one red light for you to discern what it is that you want. That's understandable. You are learning that you don't necessarily have to proceed on the same highway as usual when the light turns green. You have other roads you can choose from, based on what you are finding within. Those roads may not be as well-worn as your usual highway, but they can eventually offer a new and more refreshing experience because you are considering what *you* need and want, too.

—

In this moment, picture a time and place where you have fully stopped and are asking your self, "What do I want?" Maybe you can practice this here and now. You don't need to ask your self big questions; you can simply consider what you want or need in this moment.

37

Imagine putting yourself into the formula of your life.

A fellow person in self-recovery told a story about a family upset that occurred while they were on vacation. No one could agree on where to go for dinner. Different ideas were offered, but the conversation became heated as some of the family members were not getting their way. They started throwing around accusations and judgments of each other. The person telling the story tried to mediate the disagreements, but finally they all went their unhappy ways with no dinner together.

The person telling this story then asked herself, "Where was I in the formula?" She didn't mean that no one asked her. She meant that she did not stop to think about what she would like to do for dinner. She was so concerned about the intensity of the conversation that she focused fully on her family members, with no thought about what she would like to do. She realized after the fact that had she checked in with herself, she might well have spoken up or, better yet, taken herself out for the meal she wanted.

Putting yourself into the formula of your life means remembering that you are an important variable in that formula and factoring you into it. Make sure you connect with what you want, need, and believe and add that to the formula. You count. Be a part of decisions affecting your life.

—

In this moment, think of a current decision in your life that you are trying to make. What do you feel, want, and believe relative to that decision?

38

Being able to have your authentic voice is an intention of self-recovery.

Your. Authentic. Voice. Let's take a look at each of these three words and consider their relationship to self-recovery.

"Your" sets the stage well. It invites your focus on you right away. "Your" means ownership. It belongs to you.

"Voice" here means the expression of what you believe, what you have to say, what you want others to understand about you. It is about giving voice to what is important to you and what you value. First make sure *you* are listening to your voice. Pay attention to what you believe and want to say. Then, as you are ready, you can share your voice with others.

"Authentic" means that what you have to say is true for you. It is honest and genuine. You have spent time discerning what is true for you and you feel grounded in it—not militant or dogmatic, but clear and solid in what you believe and want. You don't need to defend or overexplain what you have to say. You can simply state it and own it.

Self-recovery is about developing your authentic voice. It is about kindly and compassionately turning inward, first to listen, and then to see if there are things within you that you wish to give voice to as you are ready.

—

In this moment, notice if there is something you are ready to give voice to that is authentically yours.

39

Connecting with your calm, grounded self opens the door to your health.

You may have noticed that when you are upset, it's hard to think. When you are upset, a network of nerves in your brain and body—the sympathetic nervous system—is activated so that, if necessary, you can fight or flee from danger. As your body instinctively prepares to protect itself in this way, your ability to think clearly and make good decisions diminishes. You can't access the part of your brain—the prefrontal cortex—that does the work of processing information more thoroughly and making intentional decisions.

To be able to think clearly once again, you have to tap into another part of your nervous system—your parasympathetic nervous system—which allows you to calm down and get your wits about you. If this doesn't naturally occur for you by noticing signals in your environment that show you are safe, you can also practice strategies such as deep breathing, stretching, or mindful awareness to intentionally tune into the present moment and calm your body and mind.

Self-recovery will be easier when you can find ways to calm and ground yourself. Being in a calm, grounded state allows you to pause and tune into your thoughts, feelings, and body. You can access that personal information, which is so valuable and necessary as you make changes in the direction of supporting your total health.

Being calm and grounded reduces anxious feelings. Being calm and grounded gives you more accurate perspectives that can lessen depressive thoughts. Being calm and grounded is also great for your body, lowering your blood pressure, releasing muscle tension, and improving sleep.

—

In this moment, place your feet on the floor, let go of anything in your hands, shut your eyes or soften your gaze, and give a nice, long exhale—or several.

40

Becoming self-reflective immediately helps you connect with you.

Self-reflection is about going within you. It is about stopping and paying attention to your reactions and experiences. Here are some questions you might ask yourself for self-reflection: *How was that for me? What do I think of that idea? How did I feel about that topic? How did I feel being treated that way?*

These are questions you can reflect upon, trying not to be judgmental or dismissive of you, but instead being open to whatever you hear yourself telling you. Maybe you were fine with how you were treated; maybe your feelings are hurt. Maybe you do not agree with the other person and find that a challenge; maybe you have no trouble with what they believe.

Self-reflection can be done in several ways. You can do it on your own by simply stopping and paying attention to your internal experiences. You can do it out loud with a trusted person, someone who will listen and give you space to be you. Or you can do it through writing, taking special time to explore how you are, what you want for you, and the direction you are headed.

The information you find about you through self-reflection helps you grow into self. Noticing your reactions, feelings, thoughts, and wonderings are ways to kindly connect with you. This noticing and listening is part of learning what is true for you. It is part of developing your authentic voice. It is a foundation of self-recovery.

—

In this moment, reflect on how you feel about this reading. What has come up for you as you consider this idea of self-reflection?

41

Self-recovery means restoring your connection with you.

This book of readings is about growing from codependency to self-recovery. Let's take a closer look at what self-recovery means.

Self-recovery means restoring your connection with you.

Perhaps you once had a good connection with you, and lost it. Powerful events in your life can take you away from self and may require you to be more externally focused. Traumatic events certainly are in this category. So are unexpected losses, disappointments, betrayals, or changes in life circumstances. Your balance of self and others got off, and you have not found your way back to you.

Or perhaps you have never had a strong connection with self. Maybe you were told that would be selfish. Maybe self-sacrificing was modeled for you, or it was a value in the worlds in which you grew up. Maybe your survival depended on your strong external focus. Maybe you feel uncomfortable with any attention on you, even attention you may give yourself. Maybe you just have no idea what connecting with you looks like or how it might help you.

Self-recovery means that, no matter what your path of disconnection has been, you are ready to retrieve your connection with you. Be assured that you will heal from that former path as you create internal connections that support new ways of being for you.

—

In this moment, think about how ready you are to improve your connection with you. To what extent are you ready? And why now?

42

Self-recovery means encouraging, developing, and healing your self.

You have heard the word "recovery" used to describe what happens after a disaster, an illness, or intense exercise. Recovery in these instances means to rebuild what was there as well as to strengthen systems so that they can promote new growth and withstand future stressors.

That's what you are doing with self-recovery! Once you have learned to more readily make contact with your internal world, the door is open for your healing, restoration, and growth.

You will likely need to heal in a number of ways. Old wounds or trauma may have caused you to develop protective patterns of self-abandonment that are still in play. You may have taken on family roles that involve being super-responsible. You may have been the go-to person for decades. To this day, you are expected to please others and not rock the boat.

Healing sets the stage for restoration of self. This may include restoring your sense of safety, your ability to focus and think, your ability to care for your emotions, and your sense of freedom. You can restore your body and mind to their natural level of healthy, balanced functioning. You can calm down, and breathe, and feel, and think.

And you can grow. You can not only rebuild self, but also build upon what you have recovered. You can learn new skills, take time for things you enjoy, develop healthy relationships, or try something you have always wanted to do.

—

In this moment, imagine what you might want to do with your growth through self-recovery.

43

What is involved in self-recovery?

Self-recovery sounds like a nice idea with appealing outcomes, doesn't it? But how do you do it?

Self-recovery involves four interlocking elements: self-understanding, self-awareness, self-competence, and self-attunement. Your readings from here to the end of this book will be about these four elements and how to bring them into your life.

Think of these elements as four circles arranged in a circle, overlapping each other. In the center of these interlocking elements is your relationship-with-self, which you are developing through your self-recovery work. This is your area of greatest potential growth. You can develop a secure attachment with your self. You can become your own safe haven. You can anchor your self in the safety and trust that you learn to lovingly provide for you.

The elements are in a circle because they do not work as a list. With a list, you do one thing and move on to the next. With these four elements of self-recovery, work on one element invites work on another element. Yes, you have to learn about these elements in some order. But as you become more familiar with each element, you will be working with them organically—self-understanding may invite self-competence, self-awareness may naturally evolve into self-attunement, and so on. You will see.

—

In this moment, take in these four elements involved in self-recovery. Just take them in. And imagine having a secure relationship with yourself as your ultimate outcome.

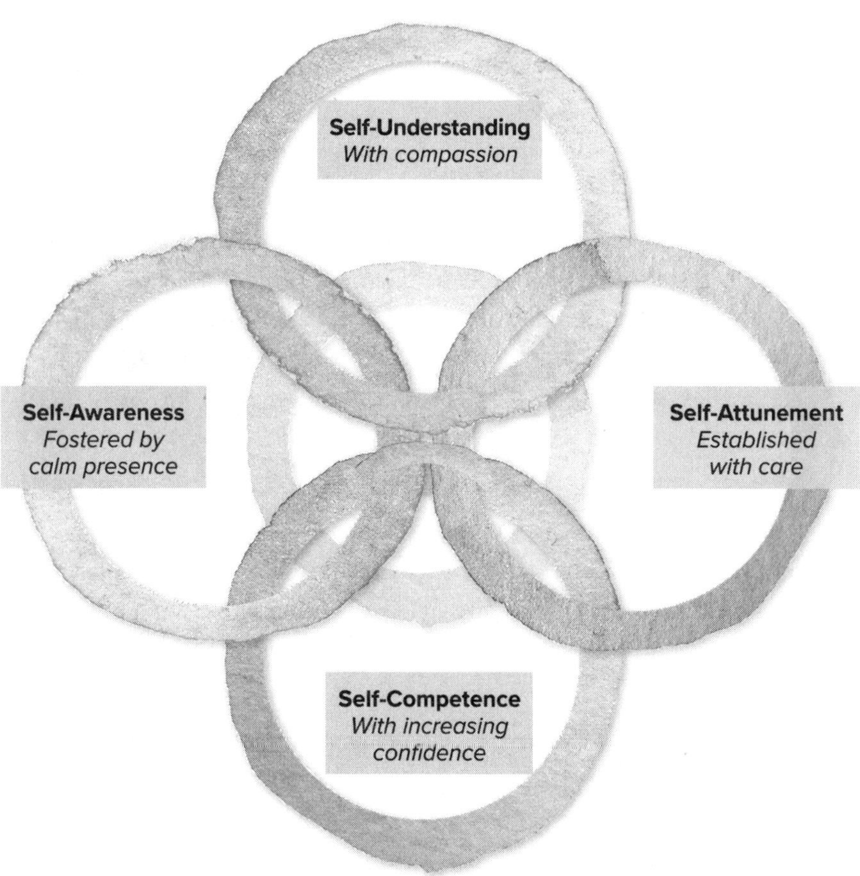
Self-Understanding
With compassion
Self-Awareness
Fostered by calm presence
Self-Attunement
Established with care
Self-Competence
With increasing confidence

44

Self-understanding with compassion is a good place to start.

You may be wondering why you are "this way." Why do you focus so much on others? Why do you find it difficult to even consider your self as you live your daily life? Why do you feel guilty for doing something for your self?

As you work with your self and codependency, you will find that self-understanding is a natural place to begin.

Self-understanding is about looking at the people, places, and things that influenced your growth over the years. It is about looking at your personal and social history through the lens of self-abandonment or self-neglect. Where did you learn to self-sacrifice? What happened that you needed to keep the focus outside of your self for safety and protection? What happened if you expressed your self?

Codependency can arise from what you learned through the modeling of others or your necessary adaptation to what you experienced in the past or in current relationships. As you come to understand more about you, you may well feel upset, disappointed, or frustrated. This is natural as you come to see and accept what is.

All of this is why it is important to bring compassion to your self-understanding. Compassion means being open and kind with your self. Offer curiosity, patience, and empathy to you. Consider your codependency as a protective part that was there to take care of you then, but may not need to be as involved now.

—

In this moment, how are you feeling about the idea of understanding your self better and being kind to you as you learn about you?

45

Self-awareness with calm presence is imperative to a safe, solid connection with you.

Self-awareness opens the door to change. Without self-awareness, you will continue in your usual patterns of daily life and interactions with others. Self-awareness is the first ingredient needed for restoring your connection to you—awareness of what you want to change in you and then awareness of the moments when you can use that personal information to speak or act in new ways.

Self-awareness is not being self-conscious—that is, the uncomfortable feeling that others are watching you and you need to do just the right thing. Self-awareness means you have calmed your self and are able to patiently notice what is going on inside of you. Calming your self gives you access to the part of your brain that helps you think more clearly and become more rational and realistic. As you quiet your emotions or impulses to act, you are better able to establish a meaningful and constructive connection with you.

Meaningful and *constructive*—such encouraging words. Meaningful in that you come to trust what you are thinking and feeling. You become curious about what you will find within you—answers you did not know were possible, ideas long pushed aside, a spark of hope and belief in you. Constructive in that, through your self-awareness with calm presence, you are building your connection with you and creating possibilities for all sorts of new growth for you.

—

In this moment, bring your self-awareness to your thoughts and feelings as you finish this reading. You might also pay attention to how your body is in this moment.

46

Self-competence with confidence is about developing new skills.

As you establish your connection with your self, you may find there are intrapersonal and interpersonal skills you lack. Intrapersonal skills are about understanding and caring for your self, while interpersonal skills are about communicating and being in relationship with others (while still honoring your self).

Growing up in ways that denied self may have left you uncertain of how to assert your self or set boundaries. Shame and guilt may be regular companions of yours and you have no idea what to do with them. You may wonder how to handle the grief you are experiencing as you make changes or how to tolerate the frustrations that arise in your life.

What you learned about communication was likely modeled for you by others in your family, school, and community. The ways people around you expressed their emotions and dealt with conflict were all you had to go on, and those ways may have been rough and rowdy or stilted and ingenuine.

Self-recovery is about learning how to be responsive, not reactive, but how can you be responsive if you don't know how to express your self and manage the guilt that may follow? How can you grow out of shame and then set healthy boundaries that kindly consider you?

This is all new territory. As you learn these skills needed for your deeper changes, you will learn how to speak and act on your own behalf. Over time, you will feel stronger and more confident because you know how to handle things that arise within you and in your relationships.

—

In this moment, can you identify one particular intrapersonal or interpersonal skill you want to develop for your self? "I sure wish I knew how to . . ."

47

Self-attunement with care pulls self-recovery together.

Self-attunement may be a new word to you. It is a word that evolved as self-recovery has evolved. Self-attunement means you really pay attention to what is going on within you. It involves more careful listening and discernment than self-awareness alone.

Think about how a person tunes a guitar or violin. It requires listening closely and making tiny adjustments that help the instrument make the exact pitch they intend for playing it.

Self-attunement is about learning to do this same thing with your self. When you self-attune, you make sure you are hearing your self correctly; you listen within for clarification of the message you are receiving from your self and what you may want to do with it. This tuning requires attention, patience, and discernment. It begins with caring about you and flourishes as you bring compassion, openness, and kindness to it.

Self-attuning may be as new to you as if someone put a guitar in your hands for the first time and asked you to tune it. You will learn how to do it and smile at the sounds of you—not flat or sharp, but clear and accurate.

As the fourth element of self-recovery, self-attunement pulls together all of your self-recovery work. It links with the other three elements—self-understanding, self-awareness, and self-competence—to create the circle-of-self-recovery map, reminding you that your work will be both specific and organic. You will explore and learn, practice and grow, moving from one element to another as helps you.

—

In this moment, identify something you can fine-tune today—a musical instrument, a dial, a scale, a digital image you are creating—and notice the attention and care this requires of you.

48

At the heart of your work is fostering your relationship-with-you.

Within the center of the four interlocking elements of self-recovery lives your relationship-with-self. This is where all of your work is directed.

You have relationships with all sorts of people in your life—family, friends, coworkers, and even acquaintances like your hairstylist or your barista. You are probably kind and considerate to them all. You probably give them attention, respect, and love. Self-recovery is about learning how to have that same type of supportive relationship with your self. Imagine that!

As you grow through self-recovery, you come to understand your self more compassionately, become more self-aware, and learn new skills to help you express your self and set healthy boundaries. You have a healthy focus on you. You are aware of when you are paying attention to others to the exclusion of your self, and you will know what to do to find balance.

In addition, as you add self-attunement to this formula for growth, you can develop a secure attachment with your self. This secure attachment is what fosters your relationship-with-self and is the ultimate goal in self-recovery. When you become attuned and responsive to your self on a consistent basis, you can count on you. You offer yourself the security and safety you seek from others and become your own safe haven. You trust your relationship with you. You are your own dear friend, teacher, parent, therapist, and guide.

—

In this moment, see if you can say something empathetic and supportive to your self, something that you might say to a dear friend who is making changes in their life.

49

You will be changing old patterns and creating new neural pathways.

Let's talk a bit about neurobiology.

You have routine ways you think about things, get things done, and interact with various people. You also have habitual ways you react to things—fears that arise, frustrations that just won't go away, hopes and dreams you've put on hold, expectations you believe others have of you.

Self-recovery is not only about becoming aware of your patterns. It is about creating new ways to think, feel, and act. Habits are not just behaviors we do. They are behaviors based in neurobiology—that is, in our brain circuitry. When you do things long enough, you create a neural pathway that makes specific behaviors and thoughts more automatic and natural, whether they are positive or negative.

People say that sidewalks are sometimes built based on the patterns first worn on the earth by people going from one point to another. Those worn pathways indicated the place for a sidewalk, an even more substantial, fixed path. So it is with your behaviors and your brain. You have substantial "sidewalks" in there that mark your familiar and preferred way of getting places. Your sidewalks are so well-worn that you don't even have to think about where you are going or how to get there.

But are you happy with where these paths take you? Is it time to pay attention to that walkway, step off the concrete path, and start creating new paths through the grass and trees? New paths are possible. It may take some weed whacking and clearing brush, but you can do it.

New neural pathways are what deep change is all about.

—

In this moment, consider a habit or pattern of behavior of yours that you would like to change.

50

How ready are you to do this self-recovery work?

Clearly, you have readiness to grow from codependency to self-recovery. You bought this book and are giving time to this reading. Please credit your self for moving forward on your own behalf!

But change challenges all of us. We have good energy and interest as we begin a new path. We buy the books, get the necessary equipment, tell our friends excitedly about what we are going to do . . . and then ambivalence steps in. *Ambivalence* means having an assortment of feelings about something. We want to move toward and away from something. As we absorb the realities of what our change involves, we may slow down or possibly give up—either by choice or by just losing steam.

This reading is inviting you to go deeper in your awareness of your readiness for self-recovery. Whether you understand what this is all about or it's too new to grasp completely, stop and listen to you. How much do you want to have a better balance of care of you and others? How interested are you in how you feel and think? Does listening to you seem like it could help? Are you ready to learn new skills to help you take care of you and express your self?

If it helps, you can rate your level of readiness using a scale of 0–10. Zero means just that: not ready. Ten means fully on board. And then there are all those numbers in between for you to pick from.

—

In this moment, sit with the number you selected as your readiness for self-recovery. How do you feel about that number? Why did you select it?

51

What ingredients will you need to cook up these self-restorative changes?

There are three ingredients you will need to begin your self-recovery work: awareness, willingness, and intentionality.

Awareness is the first and most important one. Awareness opens the door to change. Without awareness, you operate in your same-old-same-old ways. You live in your habits, your patterns of thought, emotions, and behaviors. You speak without thinking. You jump in to help when you have not been asked. You say yes when you want to say no. You pick the same type of person to be in a relationship with.

Awareness comes as you get to know your self. It comes as you learn to calm your body and think more clearly. It comes as you consider your self as much as you consider others. Awareness can stop you when you are about to do what you usually do, giving you the chance to do something different in that moment.

Willingness means you are not only aware, but you want to make a change. Sometimes you will have to look closely at your willingness. It may not be 100 percent. If that's the case, good on you for knowing that; you can instead explore your reluctance or resistance. That will help you understand you more.

Intentionality comes next. It means you are aware, willing, and now ready to do something on purpose to practice the change you want for you. Intention sets you up for taking action on something that you are committed and ready to do for you.

—

In this moment, check to see if you have these three ingredients needed for change. If not all, which do you have?

Readings on

Self-Understanding with Compassion

52

You are invited to be compassionate with your self.

This is the first of many readings about self-understanding with compassion. As you spend time in this self-understanding section, bringing compassion along with you is super important.

Codependent people can be so hard on themselves. Driven by wanting to fix things, please others, manage situations, or simply do a really great job on something, it's easy for a codependent person to feel they have failed when they are not able to do these things. "That was stupid of me." "Someone should smack me." "I'll never learn." Such expressions of self-judgment and outright self-attack are not unusual statements that codependent people may say about or to themselves.

As you read this, you probably have enough objectivity to see how talking to your self this way is hurtful. You would not talk to a child, partner, or friend this way. You know the dark power of such messages and are careful not to deliver them to others. Your self-recovery depends on not delivering them to your self, as well.

Instead, cultivate kindness and openness with your self. You will learn things that may disappoint or upset you. When this happens, be patient and supportive with your self as you look honestly at you, others in your life, and choices you have made. Being compassionate with your self invites change. Give your self credit for the efforts you made in the past, knowing you meant no harm, and honor the things you are now learning and doing differently. Compassion can help keep change humming along.

—

In this moment, think of someone or something you feel compassionate toward. What does compassion feel like?

53

Codependency may be your default mode.

Default mode means a device reverting automatically to a preselected option. You are likely familiar with this term through computer use. Unless we input something different, the computer will automatically do it the way it is programmed.

The word "programmed" is important here. Without your awareness, codependency may have been set up as your default mode. Focusing more on others may have been your way of being for many years. You may have learned early on that keeping a watchful eye or taking care of others was a good way to be. You may have felt shame and hid that by extending your self to others. A parent may have modeled selflessness for you. Whatever the source, you were programmed to focus outside of yourself to the exclusion of focusing within. You developed a hidden default mode.

The good news is that you can reset you. You do not have to go along with your automatic settings. Now that you are aware of you and your default mode of codependency, you can consciously select new ways to say and do things. You can respond, not react. You can set boundaries like never before. You can manage your feelings and not let them run away with you.

Yes, this will take intentional work, but your default mode is not giving you a full range of ways to be with your self and with others. It is even causing you problems, sometimes. Wouldn't it be nice to have more options?

—

In this moment, think of where you encounter a default mode—your computer, phone, coffeemaker. Think about the intention required to reset it, and how nice it is that you can adjust it to accommodate what you need and want.

54

Habitual patterns are worthy of noticing.

You can't change anything until you are aware of it. Habits can be especially out of your awareness. Habits are things you say or do without paying attention to them. You just do them.

For example, you may apologize reflexively before even considering whether you were at fault. You may speak in certain tones without hearing yourself. You may react habitually to certain people or situations. You may say yes, volunteer when no one else steps up, or jump in to appease a conflict without thought.

When you are acting out of habit, you are skipping thought. And thought has much to offer. It can slow you down and give you other options. It can suggest another perspective. It can give you space to simply not do anything in that moment.

The first step in shifting from habit to conscious action is becoming aware of your habits. Turning inward will help you with this. Spend time noticing your thoughts, feelings, and behaviors. Really notice the habitual ways you speak to your self or to others. Notice what you do when you feel stressed, disappointed, or fearful. Notice where your mind hangs out. Notice how you spend your time. Notice what you do impulsively, without thought. Notice when you don't remember if you said or did something because you did it out of habit. Notice how you feel about all this noticing.

—

In this moment, take time to notice your present thoughts, feelings, and impulses. Are you mindlessly dwelling in some habit of yours?

55

There are many possible reasons for focusing on others.

You have your own reasons for focusing on others. Each person has a unique combination of sources for their dominant external focus, for their other-centeredness. People develop codependency in response to a variety of life experiences.

You may be focused on others because you are kind and thoughtful. You may feel comfortable tending to others and enjoy the human connection that comes from helping and serving.

You may have been taught to focus on others, to not be selfish, to consider others first. These lessons may have been modeled for you by a parent or may have been taught directly through words and expectations.

You may have grown up in a stressful environment where you needed to be on guard most of the time. You learned that to protect your self, it was best not to be seen or heard. So, you disappeared your self. Codependency is one way to do that. By focusing on others, pleasing them, and meeting their expectations, you cannot be seen. You—a separate, whole person—are not present. Instead, you become an extension of the other person.

It is important to remember that focusing on others is not bad in and of itself. Some of the things you were taught are good for healthy relationships. Self-protection was wise and imperative. The problem comes when your focus on others causes you to lose your self. But you are here now learning about you. You are not lost.

—

In this moment, appreciate that you have not lost your self in others, that you are here for you and are simply understanding more about you and your reasons for focusing on others.

56

You may have long-standing patterns of self-abandonment learned for self-protection.

As you delve further into understanding you and codependency, please know there is nothing wrong with you. Stay connected with compassion for you, especially as you look at powerful topics such as self-abandonment. You developed codependency as a way of being for real reasons that served you well in the past but maybe do not serve you so well now. That's okay. You have outgrown codependency, just as you have outgrown the clothes you wore in the fifth grade. We grow and change.

Self-abandonment is a strong word. Who wants to feel abandoned? Fear of abandonment is a common human fear; there's nothing unusual if you have it. Codependent people will often do almost anything to not be abandoned by someone else. Ironically, as we make that choice, we abandon our selves.

You abandon your self when you are unable to speak your truth, when you disregard your feelings, plans, or desires, when you say to someone else, "Whatever you want." You likely developed self-abandonment as a self-protective coping skill years ago. You did not realize it then. You would not have named it as such. You just knew you needed to step away from you in order to keep the peace with others. An idea from you would have no place. Your upset feelings would have upset others. A different point of view would have you exiled.

Some part of you wisely knew then that you being you was not okay, so you made the unconscious choice to abandon you so you would not be abandoned by people close to you. It was understandable then; perhaps it is not needed now.

—

In this moment, kindly consider why you may have a long-standing pattern of self-abandonment.

57

Feeling safe is a priority.

As you work on your self-recovery, it is imperative that you feel safe—safe from physical and sexual harm, mental and emotional abuse, and judgment, dismissiveness, or coercion of you by someone else. Your time and space are respected, and you are not made to feel bad about you.

Feeling unsafe can come from your current life experiences. It can have roots in something that happened to you a long time ago. When you feel unsafe, your body knows to take protective care of you by shutting down. You have likely heard of the fight, flight, and freeze responses to stress. The freeze response occurs in response to not feeling safe. When you freeze, it is hard to think, speak, or act, especially on your own behalf. This is why feeling safe is so important to the work you are doing for you.

So, how can you ensure you feel safe? First, as you are able, put your self in safe situations with safe people. Think of who you feel safe with and spend time with them. Think of a place that feels safe for you and go there. Carve out moments just for you when you can say and do whatever is true for you at that time. In those moments, you feel safe that you will not be judged, instructed, or interrupted as you read something of interest to you, sing a song, scream, laugh, weep, or wonder out loud about any number of things.

—

In this moment, can you think of a person you feel safe with? Can you think of a place where you feel safe to be you?

58

Who you are has been influenced by a number of things in your life.

As you work on self-understanding, you will be looking at several sources of influence on your self-development, especially exploring where you learned to focus so much on other people and not enough on you.

There are three areas of influence in your life you will come to understand: individual, family, and social/cultural. Think of these three areas as concentric circles nesting within each other. The center circle represents your individual qualities. These qualities include your innate characteristics—the tendencies you were born with and naturally operate from.

Your individual circle is encircled by your family influences. What happened to you while you were growing up is certainly a factor in who you are today—no blame, just the truth. As you get to know you, it is valuable to understand both your nature and the nurture you received and the ways they influence your self/other balance.

The third concentric circle, which creates the outer ring, represents the social, cultural, political, and religious worlds you grew up in. The values and tenets of these broader worlds influenced your family and were taught to you.

Each person's set of concentric circles is unique. Each person is their own being with their own life experiences. Codependency does not have one particular source. It is the combination of these influences that makes you who you are today and can point the way to changes you want for you.

—

In this moment, simply let this image of influences on your self-development seep in.

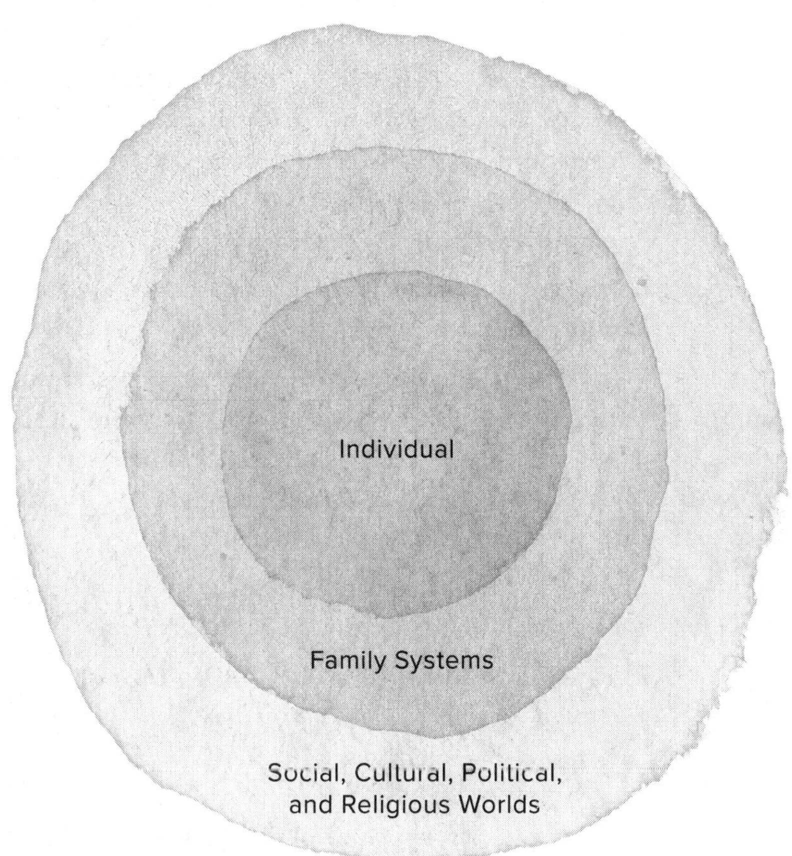
Individual
Family Systems
Social, Cultural, Political,
and Religious Worlds

59

Some of your natural tendencies may be part of your codependent ways.

Looking at your individual qualities can help you understand your strong preference to extend your self to others. Individual qualities include your basic nature and innate tendencies. You cannot fully separate these natural traits from the nurture you received, but it is valuable to name and own some of your core features so you can then embrace and parent them.

Remember, there is no blame or shame here. The mission is simply to understand you better so you can make conscious choices about the extent to which you give your self away.

Maybe you are thoughtful and sensitive by nature. Maybe you naturally care a lot about others and compassionately engage in the world. Maybe you are a natural problem-solver or fixer. Perhaps you are organized, reliable, or responsible. You like to get things done and know how to make that happen. People can count on you.

Maybe you have a strong need to control people and situations. Maybe you feel best when things are done your way and in your timeframe.

Your basic nature may have some anxiety within it. Anxiety can be a driver of codependency. Maybe you worry more than you would like to. Maybe not knowing something or having to wait makes you uncomfortable, and you are inclined to jump in when it is not yours to say or do. Perhaps your anxiety shows up in obsessive thinking or compulsive behaviors.

Any of the traits you identify as true for you are not bad. In fact, most are good . . . up to a point.

—

In this moment, notice what natural tendencies of yours come to mind.

60

What happened to you growing up is super important to who you are today.

You have natural tendencies that are personal to you, innate traits and qualities you were born with. But your individual features have been strongly influenced by the parenting and teaching you received. Some of your traits were encouraged; some were discouraged; some were judged. In response, you developed some of your qualities, discouraged others, and cut off those that did not serve you well as a child.

You learned what was okay and not okay about you from how people treated and reacted to you. If you were positively rewarded for something, you did it more; if you were treated poorly or punished for something, you did it less or hid it from those who disapproved or harmed you.

All of this affected your connection with your self. You had to edit, modify, neglect, or ignore some of your natural spark and wisdom. As you made these accommodations, you tucked pieces of you away from you. By doing this, you pleased and accommodated others or stayed out of harm's way, but your sense of self escaped you. Your sense of self is all that could escape then, but hopefully its escape is not needed now as you choose to be in safe places with safe people who are genuinely interested in who you fully are.

—

In this moment, think about a natural characteristic of you that you have not encouraged because it might get you in trouble or would disappoint others if you showed it. Then think about a natural tendency of yours that was encouraged and that you still lean into today.

61

Sometimes family rules—spoken or not—limit our connection with our self.

Rules are everywhere. Rules let us know what is expected and what is not allowed: "Stay off the grass." "Stop." "Stay in your seat." "Get in line." Rules create order. Sometimes we are not happy about the rules, but we know they keep us safe and keep things running effectively.

There were rules in the homes we grew up in. Some of those rules were spoken—"Be nice to your brother." "Don't put your elbows on the table." "Bedtime is at 10 p.m."

Other rules in the household were unspoken, but you knew they were there: *Don't upset your father. Don't mention your mother's drinking. Don't talk about what happened yesterday. Don't cry about that. Don't rock the boat. Don't leave the family.*

Believe it or not, these family rules were in place to keep things "normal." A family is a system and seeks to maintain the status quo, whatever it looks like for that family. Unfortunately, some status quos are not healthy and restrict the growth of each person.

Whether spoken or not, the family rules you lived with may have limited yourself-awareness and self-expression. You learned to not talk about what was really going on at home. You ignored the behaviors of certain people and worked around them. You knew your feelings had no place in the house, so you stuffed them down or acted them out. You learned to not trust others or your self.

—

In this moment, consider whether you are still living by your family of origin's rules. If so, are those rules keeping you from hearing your self, saying how you feel, or trusting others?

62

You likely took on at least one family role to keep peace in your family.

Each person in a family has a role or two. They have probably not been "officially" assigned. Each person simply took on the jobs necessary to maintain the family's status quo, to try to keep things from going off the rails (even if they were already off the rails).

Roles can include keeping everyone happy, making your family proud, seeing that everyone is taken care of, or making personal adjustments so that no one gets upset, especially with you. Keeping to yourself, not asking for anything, or always deferring to someone else are also roles, as are acting out and causing problems for the family.

Whatever roles you may have taken on, it is important to know that they served you well at that time. Your roles protected you, gave your life some definition, and helped you live with your family of origin with as little upset as possible.

The problem with roles is that they may have served you well in the past but tend to not serve you as well in the present. Without awareness, you may be playing out your familiar, well-rehearsed roles that support your codependency, roles that have you taking care of and pleasing others while neglecting your self. The role itself is not bad or wrong. It is a problem, though, if that is the only role you can play.

—

In this moment, consider what roles you took on in childhood and are very good at still. Are they your dominant roles? Bringing your roles into awareness will help you choose whether to play those roles yet again or try something different.

63

Attachment styles can be a factor in codependency.

An attachment style is characterized by the ways you feel, think, and behave in your relationships. We all have basic needs for a secure relationship in which we feel safe, confident, and protected. The attachment style you developed depends on how well those needs were fulfilled when you were a child.

If your caregivers were attuned and responsive to you consistently, you likely developed a secure attachment style. You could count on them to provide safety and security. You developed trust and confidence in self and others. Your caregivers were a secure base from which you could comfortably explore the world.

If your caregivers were not attuned, responsive, or predictable in how they treated you, you likely developed an insecure attachment style, a style that makes it more difficult for you to trust and connect safely with others or your self. This is where codependency comes in.

An insecure attachment style can be a source of codependency.

An insecure attachment style can make you unnecessarily focused on others—to please them, quiet your worries, or find reassurance that your relationship with them is still intact. An insecure attachment style can cause you to overfunction for others and underfunction for self. You believe you are valued for what you can do for the other person, not for your worthiness and lovability.

Insecure attachment styles are about seeking outside of self the safety and security you naturally desire and need.

—

In this moment, think about the caregiving you received. Did you feel seen and loved for who you are? Could you trust your parents to be there for you, no matter what?

64

An insecure anxious attachment style may have you fearful of abandonment.

An insecure anxious attachment style can develop if you received inconsistent care from your primary caregivers. Perhaps what they offered you ranged from appropriate to harmful. Never knowing what to expect from your caregivers, you became anxious and preoccupied with doing things to reassure your self about the security of your connection with them.

This attachment style can leave you fearful of abandonment. Set in childhood, this fear can show up in your adult relationships. You worry about being left by the other person. You do many things to keep from being rejected, such as making extra efforts to please them or do things for them. You deny your own voice and preferences in order to ensure they will stay with you.

An insecure anxious attachment style can also involve often seeking validation and reassurance from important others in your life. Not secure within your self, you seek to build your sense of self from what others can offer you.

To complicate the picture, codependent people with an insecure anxious attachment style too often seek this validation from people who are not able or willing to give such reassurance. An entanglement ensues. The codependent person, still needy of this external validation, further pursues reassurance with this person who is unable to provide the secure relationship they continue to seek. Ironically, this pursuit can result in the very abandonment the codependent person fears.

—

In this moment, consider if you have an insecure anxious attachment style. Are you worried about being abandoned? Do you need the validation of someone else to feel good about you?

65

An insecure avoidant attachment style may have you managing and controlling others.

An insecure avoidant attachment style can develop if you did not experience your primary caregivers as emotionally available to you. Your caregivers were not able to validate and respond to your feelings and may have discouraged you from needing anything from them. You were encouraged to take care of your own needs. You formed no attachment with your primary caregivers and kept your distance—emotionally and physically.

Carrying this insecure avoidant attachment style into your adult relationships, you may avoid intimacy and be fiercely independent. You may find it hard to trust others; you may be unwilling to even try. You protect your vulnerability by being overly involved in the lives of others, not giving space or time to your own. You may be controlling of people and situations in order to have things as you need them to be so that you can feel safe.

You can hear the echoes of codependency in this description of insecure avoidant attachment style: *Focus on others. Controlling. Self-sufficient.* Yes, codependency can involve many controlling behaviors. Cloaked in caregiving and problem-solving, managing and controlling others may well be the more fundamental need of the codependent person. With early injuries that left them with an insecure avoidant attachment style, the codependent person continues to protect themselves from closeness by taking on the roles of manager and controller. These roles can establish a safe—but not intimate—relationship.

—

In this moment, consider if you have an insecure avoidant attachment style. Are you aware of being self-sufficient or keeping your distance? Are you aware of being controlling? If so, what purpose does it serve for you?

66

A secure attachment comes from feeling heard and responded to on a consistent basis.

Most of us want to feel safe and secure in our relationships. We don't want to feel anxious about whether someone likes us or worried about whether they are soon to leave us. We want to feel free to be our self, respecting the other person as we wish to be respected by them. All of this describes a secure attachment.

We can develop a secure attachment from primary caregivers who were sensitive and responsive to us on a consistent basis. They responded to our natural needs for safety, security, and protection. We knew we could count on them, and that helped us trust others. We developed an internal security that gave us confidence, comfort, and the ability to grow.

Having a secure attachment style is a foundation for your total health. Who wouldn't want internal security and the ability to grow? Perhaps you received kind, supportive care from your primary caregivers or others in your life. Perhaps you have a secure attachment style now.

Perhaps you used to have a secure attachment style, but you seem to have lost your connection with your internal security. Certain relationships can disrupt your sense of security. So can jobs, community involvement, or health concerns. Instead of feeling comfortable and confident in your own skin, you now feel upset and preoccupied. Codependent behaviors have set in, and you wonder what happened to the you that used to feel secure and connected.

—

In this moment, imagine what a secure attachment style feels like. Are you familiar with it? Have you had it in the past? Would you like to have a secure attachment going forward?

67

Trauma survival naturally involves disconnection from self.

Trauma involves having experienced, witnessed, or been repeatedly exposed to events that involved actual or threatened death or serious injury. Relational trauma comes from attachment wounds that cause insecure attachment styles. Complex trauma is caused by one person harming, violating, or exploiting another human being. Often, the experiences of complex trauma have been repetitive, prolonged, and perpetrated by caregivers while raising their children. Such traumatic experiences include physical, emotional, or sexual abuse, neglect, humiliation, or discrimination. Other experiences associated with complex trauma include growing up in homes with addiction, domestic violence, mental illness, or poverty.

A fundamental consequence of trauma is damage to self. If your sense of self was constantly under fire, you rightfully protected your self from others and from you. You disconnected from you. You abandoned your self-awareness, knowledge, expression, confidence, and trust. You did this because you had to.

Disconnection from self plants the seeds of codependency in some people. Trauma puts you on guard and creates a necessary foundation for external focus. This focus helps you survive, but it does not give you the space for self-awareness and self-consideration. As you become programmed to watch outside of your self to ensure your safety, approval, and love, you cannot develop your internal focus. There's just no time, space, brain, or heart for doing so.

—

In this moment, whether you have experienced trauma or not, consider how natural it is for a person who feels threatened or demeaned to develop a strong focus on others for self-protection.

68

Healing from trauma makes healing from codependency possible.

Trauma can be so powerful that sometimes injuries from it have to be addressed before you can work on your codependency. Your self-protection may be so strong that any efforts you make to connect within may be met with guilt, fear, resistance, or doubt. Old messages warning you not to be selfish may surface. Well-worn patterns of hypervigilance may still be present and exhausting and make focusing on your self close to impossible. Self-protection runs long and deep for good reasons.

Addressing trauma means a couple of things. First, if it is your life experience, acknowledge that what happened to you was traumatic. This willing awareness opens the door to your healing. Perhaps you can do this acknowledgment with a therapist who specializes in trauma treatment. If you don't already have one, you will likely benefit from finding such a therapist. Fortunately, many therapists are now qualified to do trauma-informed work.

As you work on the effects of trauma on your life, your adaptive self-protection will become quieter. Focusing on others won't be your automatic, go-to way of being. You will know better how to work with your self-protection so you can have more access to you. You will feel more comfortable being still and connecting within. Your growth from codependency to self-recovery will then be able to move forward more fully and successfully.

—

In this moment, consider whether your self-protection by focusing on others keeps you from kindly and comfortably going within. Might this be a trauma response you could address?

You have many parts.

We each have a variety of parts in us, and we often think and speak about them naturally—for example, "Part of me wants to go out tonight, and part of me just wants to stay in." Your parts developed in response to your life experiences growing up and in adulthood. Your parts emerged from your family rules and roles, your attachment style, and trauma. They are responses to the ways you have been treated in your intimate relationships, work settings, and community.

Your parts may be encouraging, creative, ambivalent, or counterproductive. They each serve a specific protective role, and it is worth getting to know each of them. Some examples of protective parts include child parts—parts of you that are needy, afraid, or a troublemaker. You also have adult parts—parts of you that are wise and strong. Your emotions can be seen as parts—shame, guilt, fear, hope, regret. Your thoughts are also parts of you—messages such as *I am no good* or *I am not worth caring about.* Even your behaviors are parts—the parts of you that stay busy, hide out, or scramble to keep the peace.

Why is getting to know your parts with compassion worthwhile? Because self-recovery is about developing your relationship-with-self. Each of your parts is part of your self. As your parts learn to live together in your community of self, your authentic, stable, workable relationship with you can grow.

—

In this moment, take in this idea of you having many parts. We all do. There is no need to be concerned about having a variety of parts within you giving you an assortment of messages.

70

Some of your protective parts make it hard to connect with your self.

Self-recovery is about improving your self/other balance. This involves increasing your ability to go within you and be with whatever you may find there. Going within can be more of a challenge than you think. It's a nice idea, but lo and behold, all sorts of parts can show up and make it difficult for you to be still and be with you.

The parts that show up are protective, so you don't want to chase them away. You really can't, anyway. What they are protecting you from depends on your story, but in general, they may be protecting you from your feelings, from speaking up, or from taking action on your own behalf—anything that your past experiences taught them may not be safe for you.

Parts that are restless or productivity-oriented may be protecting you from previous emotional or physical harm. They are hypervigilant, always scanning for the next thing coming your way. They believe that sitting quietly with your self is dangerous.

Perhaps your protective parts show up as a blank mind, low energy, or numbness. These parts, too, have programming from the past that blocks you now from actively getting to know your self. So, when you pause to connect with you—maybe even when you read the reflection at the end of each reading—you space out or skip it because you really don't want to go there just yet. That's okay. Just notice your community of parts in action.

—

In this moment, do you notice any parts showing up that are making it hard for you to be with you?

71

Hearing from your parts requires safety, patience, and compassion.

Whether your parts show up as child parts, adult parts, emotions, thoughts, or behaviors, it is most helpful to greet them with kindness and curiosity. It's unlikely you would greet even a stranger at your door with "What do you want?!" or "Go away." Unless you knew them to be dangerous, you would probably say in a neutral voice, "How can I help you?"

Your parts protect you, but they may be strangers to your conscious awareness. To build a solid relationship with them, it is important to meet and greet them, asking, "What would you like for me to know about you? What is it you want from me?" By creating a back-and-forth dialogue, you are more likely to learn how to respond to your parts so they don't overwhelm or dominate you.

This internal dialogue will happen only if you feel safe and convey safety to your parts. This means you are physically and emotionally safe, and you can reassure the part that you will not shout at it or drive it away.

Patience is also needed as you listen to your parts and start to understand each other. That's how most relationships are. Whether those relationships are with family, friends, partners, or pets, it takes many conversations and shared experiences to really know each other.

Compassion for your self and your parts is what makes your relationship with your community of parts possible. Kindness and openness foster the internal connections you are building for you.

—

In this moment, see if you can meet and greet a part of you that is showing up right now.

72

Where in the world did you learn that?

Probably sometime in your life someone has asked you, "Where in the world did you learn that?" Usually this is asked with curiosity and a bit of surprised wondering. In addition to our families, we learn things from the broader social, cultural, political, and religious environments we grow up in. What you learn in these broader worlds—the values and tenets that are taught to you directly or indirectly—influences your self-development.

Specific to codependency, where in the world did you learn to focus more on others without consideration of you? Where did you learn that self-care was selfish? Where did you learn that your having an idea or an opinion had no place? Who taught you to be seen and not heard? What broader-world messages kept you from believing in your own possibilities?

Each school, religion, community, political organization, and government has its own set of beliefs, its own reasons for those beliefs and a unique logic that results from them, its own ways those beliefs are acted upon and encouraged in others. This is not necessarily to blame your broader worlds for the imbalance between your care of self and your care for others. It is just to become aware of the sources of influence on your thoughts, feelings, and actions and who you have become.

—

In this moment, consider what broader-world influences in your life might be sources of your other-centeredness.

73

You can determine what you do and don't want to keep from what you were taught.

The influences of communities and organizations such as schools, religious groups, neighborhoods, and governments have profoundly affected who you are today. Those broader worlds have been the water in which you swam, the air you breathed. They created order and likely taught you things that have been helpful along the way. But maybe you wish to consider whether the beliefs, rituals, roles, and rules of those worlds serve you now as you continue to grow.

Staying with what you were taught and learned is certainly a fine choice if those influences are working for you. Perhaps they give you a foundation for a life you like. Perhaps you believe deeply in the things you were taught. It's good to be aware of your reasons to keep these influences as part of who you are.

You can also choose to let go of any beliefs and norms of your formative worlds that do not fit with who you are now or who you are becoming. The twelve-step programs say about their program, "Take what you like and leave the rest." You have this choice with what life has taught you, too.

Your awareness of these influences comes first. Next, bring to mind the changes you want for you, the ways you want to respect and encourage your self as you live with and love others. In order to become the person you want to be, you may have to let go of old beliefs that restrict you—and create new messages that recognize and free you in fresh new ways. With due respect for your past teachers, you can welcome a new teacher: you.

—

In this moment, notice if any past lessons from your school, church, or other communities make it hard for you to consider your self more.

74

Learning about your self may bring you down.

As you grow in self-understanding, you may find a heaviness within. Allowing your self to see and accept the realities of your life can be freeing, but first grief may set in. This is normal.

Grief is associated with more than just death. It can be a response to the loss of anything important to you, including dreams, hopes, and expectations. As you are learning about your tendencies to focus too much on others, you may have become more aware of how your experiences growing up contributed to your self/other imbalance. This may have changed how you see the people and community who raised you.

As you understand the family roles you took on or the trauma you have experienced, you may be ready to make changes in you that will involve letting go of some of your familiar thoughts, feelings, and behaviors so you can grow. This, too, is loss.

Grief can present itself in a number of ways, including denial, depression, and anger. Anxiety can increase with grief as well—as you let go of one thing, the unknown appears, and worry and fear step in. However your grief shows itself, know that it is normal and natural for the growth you seek. As you grow forward, you will find acceptance of your losses and good energy for the new life you are creating.

—

In this moment, notice how you are feeling about all that you are understanding about you. You probably have an assortment of feelings. Is one of them grief?

75

Allowing your grief goes a long way.

Wanting to chase your grief away is as normal as having grief in the first place. Even the word—*grief*—sounds heavy and dark. Who wants to feel heavy and dark? But here's the thing: Allowing your grief to exist diminishes its power and frees you to move on with your life.

Does that sound fantastical? Let's break this down.

Feelings are best acknowledged and experienced. Grief can involve an assortment of feelings, including denial, depression, anger, and anxiety. In other words, you are not having multiple problems—your feelings associated with grief can be different each day or even each hour, and they like to be recognized.

Allowing your feelings of grief is best done with safe people in safe places. You might take a bit of time to decide who these safe people and places are. Safe people are those who can sit with you and your grief without wanting to fix it or make it go away. These people support your growth. Safe places are locations where you won't be interrupted and won't be heard by unsupportive people. These places give you a sense of peace and centeredness.

You are doing an amazing job of sticking with your program for self-recovery. Grief is a necessary part of making changes. Trust this process and know that as your strong feelings of grief lessen, you will be able to find meaning in your losses and a readiness for your future.

—

In this moment, if you are in a safe place, allow whatever feeling may be yours right now. Just recognize your feeling and breathe with it.

76

The better you understand you, the more you will see your strengths.

You have been doing a lot of hard work as you've read about what has influenced your self-development, especially the development of your tendencies to focus on others while neglecting your self. Through this exploratory work, you can also identify the personal strengths that supported you in the past and upon which you can build for the future.

Strengths can be found in your basic nature, in the family roles you took on, in what helped you to survive, in your parts of self, and in benefits from the broader worlds in which you grew up.

Strengths in your nature may include kindness, sensitivity, patience, or tenacity.

Strengths from your family roles may include being organized, good at decision-making, self-disciplined, calm in upsetting situations, honest, or creative. If you lived with trauma, you certainly have strengths within that helped you to survive, such as resourcefulness, determination, and hopefulness. You know how to protect your self and others.

Your parts are also strengths. You have adult parts, wise parts, and other allies within. These parts know you and are waiting for you to remember and call upon them. Even your child parts have strengths such as playfulness and spontaneity.

And no doubt you gained strengths from the broader worlds in which you have lived. The influences from schools, churches, or other communities may have given you social skills, compassion, insight, or spirituality.

Maybe you have been noticing your strengths. Maybe there are more within you for you to discover and welcome.

—

In this moment, name at least one of your strengths and feel that strength as you identify it.

77

Staying connected with your strengths is part of self-recovery.

Stay in touch with your strengths as you move forward in your self-recovery. Encourage them and build on them. Self-recovery is about both *retrieving* your self when you have lost your self in someone else and *restoring* your self to health. Self-recovery is about having a strong enough connection with you that you more naturally balance your focus between others and your self.

Staying connected with your strengths is a deep part of your self retrieval and restoration. If you only see your flaws and problems, you limit your growth. Such a focus influences how you feel about your self and likely keeps you down and stuck.

Telling you about your strengths is not just the stuff of happy greeting cards. You have strengths you are using to read this book—diligence, curiosity, openness, hopefulness, courage. Pay attention to how your strengths show up in your day. Notice how you use them or not. If you don't use them, notice what kept you from being, for example, courageous, funny, or insightful. If you did lean into your strengths, notice how that felt and what happened when you did.

If your strengths are not naturally showing up in a situation, remember that you have them, and call on them. Connect with your wise self who can guide you. Connect with your adult parts that can lovingly help your child parts. Find an ally within for comfort and support. Your team of strengths are ready and waiting for you to engage with them.

—

In this moment, identify a strength that has kept you reading this book on codependency recovery.

78

Careful: Your strengths can become your weaknesses.

With all of this good being said about your strengths, it is important to be careful how far you engage them. Codependent people are loaded with strengths in caregiving, fixing, problem-solving, managing, and making things happen. You may be good at these things and naturally jump in. But you can carry your strengths too far. This is when codependency comes into play.

As you over-engage your strengths, they can shift from being assets to causing problems for you and others. If you are good at managing things but take the work of others out of their hands, your strengths have now caused you problems. If you love to caregive and insist on doing so after someone has declined your help, you are injuring your relationship. If you are trying to fix something no one else sees as a problem, you will be frustrating everyone, including your self.

Use your strengths to help you connect with you and accomplish what you want for you. Your strengths are not there for you to save the world—or at least, not until you have saved *you*. Pay attention to when your strengths have carried you into relationship entanglements, pull them back, and see how you can enlist them to help you with your self-recovery instead. As you continue in your healing, you will learn how to maximize your strengths without losing your self in the process.

—

In this moment, think of one of your strengths that can carry you into a relationship entanglement if you are not careful. Then think of how you can use that same strength on your own behalf.

Readings on

Self-Awareness with Calm Presence

79

Being aware of your body, mind, emotions, and spirit is essential to self-recovery.

Remember that the four elements of self-recovery—self-understanding, self-awareness, self-competence, and self-attunement—are intersecting circles forming a larger circle. The elements overlap each other, illustrating the ways one element affects other elements. In the previous set of readings, you spent time with self-understanding with compassion; you can now build on your self-understanding by adding the second element of self-recovery: self-awareness with calm presence.

Self-awareness opens the door to change. Without self-awareness, you are not present in the moments when you are about to do the same old thing that entangles you. You miss the moment when you have said enough and should stop. You miss the moment to speak up. You say yes when you want to say no. You offer to help when you have no extra time. You take over and hurt someone else's feelings.

Adding self-awareness gives you the choice in the moment between doing what you usually do and doing something new and different.

You develop self-awareness in four areas of self: body, mind, emotions, and spirit. Think of these four areas as another set of intersecting circles. As with the elements of self-recovery, these four areas of self influence each other tremendously. What you think affects how you feel. Your body absorbs how you feel. Your spirit can quiet your mind and emotions.

Self-awareness is a gentle presence that allows you to notice what is going on within you. Those things are going on whether you are aware or not. It's better to be aware.

In this moment, bring one thing into your awareness from one of your four areas of self: body, mind, emotions, or spirit.

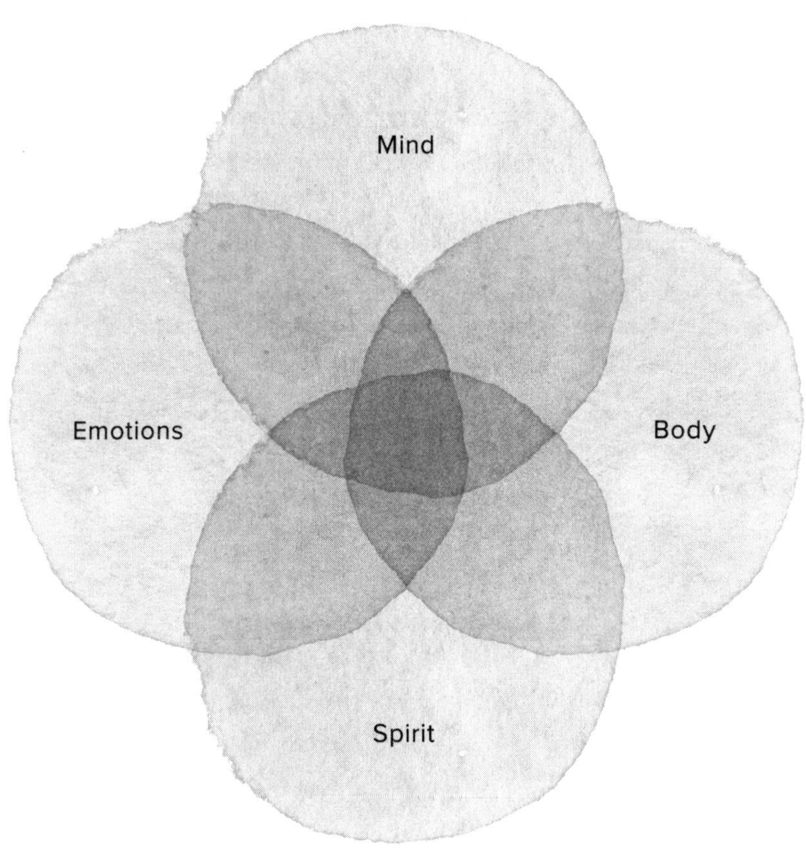
Mind
Emotions
Body
Spirit

80

Having a calm presence is what makes self-awareness possible.

Just as the four areas of self—body, mind, emotions, and spirit—interplay, so do all of the systems within your body. When you are upset, your body reacts by setting off protective behaviors. You may want to fight or flee. You may freeze up. This protection happens without your conscious choice. It is a natural way your system is taking care of you.

What happens, though, is that as your body acts in these protective ways, your ability to think diminishes. The part of your brain that can assess and make good decisions is not easily accessible. The reptilian part of your brain reads the situation as danger and initiates action, not thought.

Self-awareness does not work well when you are stressed or upset. The gentle presence that allows you to notice what is going on within you is not possible. In fact, gentle presence is the opposite of an activated system that needs to protect itself.

People tell us to "calm down," but that is not something we can do on demand. It is a skill to be learned. Calming down involves noticing you are in an upset state, wanting to return to a calmer state, and then, as a starter, making a long, deep exhale several times. The calmer you become, the better able you are to restore your abilities to think, discern, and decide. Your body's system is regulating itself, and you can now more fully regulate you.

—

In this moment, make three long, deep exhales and see how that feels.

81

When you are upset, your natural fight, flight, or freeze reactions are set off.

Understanding self-awareness with calm presence is helped by first understanding what is going on neurobiologically when you are stressed, upset, or in danger.

There is a part of your brain that is responsible for your survival. It is sensitive to any threats of harm to you. It naturally reacts without your having to think about what to do. In real danger, there is no time to think. Action is needed immediately. Fight, flight, and freeze are the primary reactions your body may take in such threatening situations.

Fight means you move toward what may harm you. Your body is mobilized to strike, defend, or attack. You may feel agitated or restless. You have a strong impulse to do something to protect your self or to make the threat of danger go away.

Flight means you move away from what may harm you. Your protective response is to withdraw, hide, or disappear. You have a strong impulse to not be seen or heard in order to protect your self.

Freeze means you are immobilized. Your mind goes blank and your body is numb. Your ability to speak or act shuts down. The freeze response involves feeling unsafe, whether consciously or subconsciously. It is a survival mechanism activated when you sense danger and neither fight nor flight is possible—or when these were not options in the past, such as with childhood trauma.

It is helpful to understand these natural responses to stress and upset feelings when your codependency has you entangled and way off your center. This is what is going on in you.

—

In this moment, consider whether you are inclined to fight, flee, or freeze when you feel threatened.

Fawning and fixing are two other ways your upset self may express itself.

Often codependency begins with just trying to help someone. This is not a bad thing to do as a thoughtful human being, but if we carry our helping too far, relationship entanglements and heated upsets can ensue. You may then feel hurt, angry, frustrated, disappointed, unappreciated, or attacked. Your survival responses of fight, flight, or freeze step in, or maybe you react in one of two other protective ways: fawning or fixing.

The *fawn* reaction means you try to appease and please the threatening or abusive person. You flatter them or go to great lengths to keep them happy. You seek safety by merging your needs and wishes with the other person. Their needs become more important than your own. You let go of your boundaries in order to please them. You seek their approval and reassurance.

The *fix* reaction means you feel very strongly that you need to say and do something right away to fix the situation between you and another person. Yours is not a calm, let's-figure-this-out-together approach. Rather, your desperation has you scrambling to restore the breach you are experiencing. You feel an urgency and compulsivity that takes you deeper into your codependent ways.

Your body is wired to protect you. Yet sometimes it is overprotective of you. Self-recovery involves noticing your survival responses in action and learning how to adjust them so you can think more clearly and make conscious choices about how you want to respond, not react.

—

In this moment, consider whether you identify with fawning or fixing as a way to cope with upset feelings.

83

You can calm your self when your body has set off its alarms.

Good news! You *can* calm your self when your body has set off its alarms. It will require learning and practicing some new techniques, but it is worth it. The calm groundedness you establish for your self can be pleasant in itself, and it will help you be more self-aware. You will be better able to connect with your body, mind, emotions, and spirit.

You can have control over your strong emotions and familiar reactions. You don't have to go with your fight or flight responses. You can learn to quiet your self so that you know what you want to say and can say it in challenging situations. You don't have to freeze. You can learn how to find safety and restore your body and mind by doing so. You don't have to fawn, because you learn about your value and equality. You don't have to scramble to fix a relationship breach, because you can learn how to slow down and find resolution step-by-step, including you in each of those steps.

Alarms are useful as protective devices, but a blaring, stuck alarm is too much. You can learn how to turn off your alarm—or at least turn it way down—so you can hear yourself think and go from there.

—

In this moment, think of an alarm you are able to quiet. How do you feel when it is no longer blaring?

84

Feeling safe is the first step to calming yourself.

We don't turn off an alarm unless we are safe. You wouldn't turn off the fire alarm until the fire department had checked for fire. You wouldn't turn off a siren or emergency notification for weather until you had full information and had taken necessary protective action. So it is with quieting the alarms of fight, flight, freeze, fawn, or fix reactions. Don't try to quiet them until you feel safe.

You will be an active creator of your safety. First, try not to put your self into unsafe situations. We know when we may be walking into an interaction that threatens our emotional, mental, or physical safety. Codependency can move us toward unsafe circumstances more than is good for us. We keep wanting to help, fix, or restore a relationship that is not safe for us.

If you find your self in an unsafe situation, do your best to stop and leave. Pursuing will not likely get you what you want. You may incur further damage as you go too far.

It is also helpful to think about safe people and places in your life. Identify them in advance of feeling unsafe. Bring them to mind or go to them when you feel unsafe. Think of colors and images that feel safe to you. Soak them in. Let those images hold you and relay authentic safety.

With safety in place, your body quiets its alarms and naturally starts calming itself through another neurobiological path. Then, your efforts to calm yourself will be more effective and lasting.

—

In this moment, think of a safe person or place in your life that can be a resource for you.

85

Settle into safe stillness.

It is likely you are not used to being still. Codependency can lead us to be very active with caregiving, problem-solving, or managing others. We think we have no time for stillness. It can feel like a waste of time, or you may worry about what will happen to everyone else while you are being with you. Stillness can seem like a luxury.

But in fact, stillness is a necessity. Stillness is restorative. It restores your neurological balance of activation and calm. It regulates your breathing, heart rate, and blood pressure. It quiets your mind and relaxes your body. You can soften your strong external focus and attune to what's within. You restore your connection with you.

Becoming still is an art and a practice that first involves feeling safe. Twice each day, try to find five minutes to stop and be still in your safe place. Let your hands be free of everything, including your devices so you won't be interrupted (or interrupt your self). Simply be in silence. Allow your body to naturally settle, and invite your thoughts to give you a break. At the end of your five minutes, notice how you feel. What was that like? What challenged you in being still? What helped you to be still? Is anything different in you? Do you feel calmer? More connected to you? Just notice, without judgment. You are practicing something new. You are in a training program to develop your ability to be with you.

—

In this moment, if you can, close this book and be still for five minutes using the guidance you just read.

86

Deep, diaphragmatic breathing can tell your survival brain to calm down.

Diaphragmatic breath relays a message to the upset part of your brain that it can calm down. Simply telling that part of your brain to calm down does not work nearly as well as creating safety and settling into your diaphragmatic breath, as this practice describes:

- Find a safe place and settle into stillness. Sit in an upright posture that conveys your dignity and allows your breath to flow evenly and smoothly. Shut your eyes or gently look downward. Release your shoulders, notice your sits bones supporting you, and place your feet flat on the floor. You are grounding your self.
- Begin to follow your breath at your nose and mouth. Don't try to change the speed or depth of your breathing. Follow your natural breath, being aware of the sensations of air coming in through your nose and out through your mouth. Let your exhales become longer than your inhales. This naturally deepens your breath. With more air out, more can come in, and your breath can become deep belly breathing.
- After several minutes of this practice, shift your focus to your breath at your diaphragm. Place your hand on your diaphragm and notice its rise with your inhale and fall with your exhale. Spend some time following your diaphragmatic breath. Your mind may jump in. That's normal. When that happens, simply notice your thinking and return your focus to following your breath.
- Enjoy the natural rhythms of your breath. In and out. Deep and slow.

—

In this moment, if you wish, close this book and practice diaphragmatic breathing for a few minutes.

87

Scanning your body through your mind's eye can release tension and holding.

The body scan is a mindfulness practice that can calm and ground you. The body scan involves using your mind's eye—creating a picture in your mind—to travel from one end of your body to the other. As you do this, you notice sensations in each named part of your body and breathe mindfully in and out of that area.

Here is a practice for you.

- Find a safe place to become still. You may be seated or lying down. Gently shut your eyes or soften your gaze, and follow the in and out of your breath for a few minutes.
- Then begin your body scan by noticing the top of your head. What sensations do you feel there? What are you aware of? In your mind's eye, breathe in and out through the top of your head.
- Now shift your awareness to your neck. Notice any sensations in your neck. What are you aware of? Using your mind's eye, breathe in and out through your neck.
- Continue downward through your body using this same noticing and breath awareness for your face, shoulders, arms, hands, fingers, spine, hips, legs, feet, and toes.
- As you near the end of this practice, simply focus on your diaphragmatic breath, imagining each exhale flowing from the top of your head through your body and out through your feet, a gentle waterfall washing over and through you. Stay with your body and breathe in this way for a few minutes.

—

In this moment, if you wish, close this book and practice a body scan.

88

Stretching invites awareness and encourages release.

Simple stretching goes a long way in releasing tension and inviting self-awareness. You don't need to take a class or buy the right outfit to stretch. You can stretch right now. Let's do it!

- Stand with your feet under your hips. Soften your knees, release your shoulders, and follow your breath.
- Now, allow your head to bend forward, not forcing it but going to the edge of your stretch. Breathe in and out two times. On your next inhale, raise your head back to its centered placement and exhale. Do this neck stretch forward, back, right, and left two times. Go slowly, paying attention to your movement and breath.
- Now, circle your right arm up from your side until it is over your head. Lift your arm a bit further, and then gently tip toward your left side, carrying your arm with you. Go to the edge of your stretch and dwell there. Then, on an inhale, lift your body and arm upright and allow your right arm to gently circle back down to your side. Do this stretch on the right and left two times.
- Notice if your body is asking for another stretch and move in any way that feels good and supportive to you, remembering to move with awareness. You are cultivating calm and release in this moment, and you are training your self for the self-awareness that self-recovery thrives on.
- When you have stretched enough for now, return to your original standing position, follow your diaphragmatic breath for several cycles, and continue to release whatever you may be holding.

—

In this moment, if you wish, stand up and stretch as suggested in this reading.

89

Get up and move.

Movement is an excellent way to regulate your neurobiology from activated to calm. Most of us know this, but getting ourselves up and moving can take special effort and energy. We get stuck in our chair, on our phone, or in our mind. We keep thinking we will stop and go do something more active, but the requirements of our day make it hard to squeeze in movement. Or we are so compulsively engaged in our sedentary activities that we just can't stop ourselves.

Movement doesn't have to be heavy-duty exercise. Movement also means getting up to stretch, walk, go outside for a while, or put on some music and dance. Get your blood flowing. Oxygenate your body. Interrupt your thoughts, which may be circular and obsessive. Interrupt your emotions, which may be heavy and intrusive. Sitting with your thoughts and emotions will only keep stressing you, and your body will get tighter and weaker.

Self-awareness helps us intentionally get up and move. Recognize when you have had enough of your thinking for the day, or at least the moment. Recognize when your body is asking for activity. Notice if you are restless, stiff, or bored. Think of easy, accessible movement for you in your home or at work. Think of your preferred ways to move and do them. Don't make movement a chore that requires a big block of time and a change of clothes. Think simple and immediate.

—

In this moment, what movement can you get up and do right now? Give it a try.

90

Being in the present moment fosters self-awareness.

We get lost in thought. We live in our heads and not in the present moment. We do it a lot of the time, without thought. Our minds are ever-present in their activity. Thinking is our default way of being. Thinking serves us well *and* it can go too far. You can lose your self in your own thinking.

Being in the present moment means you notice your thinking and then shift your awareness to anything in the moment you are in. You can focus on your breath or body sensations. You can use your five senses to quiet your mind and come into the present.

Here is a practice for connecting with your self when you are lost in thought:

- Sit in stillness for several minutes, following your diaphragmatic breath. When settled, open your eyes and pick something for your eyes to focus on. Notice the colors, textures, light, and detail of what you see. Spend time there. When thoughts show up, nonjudgmentally notice them, then redirect your attention to what you are looking at.
- As you are ready, shift your awareness to your other senses one by one: sound, touch, taste, and smell. With each sense, pick something in your present environment to focus on and pay attention to the details that sense is conveying. Notice how food tastes, feel the breeze, smell your coffee.

Present-moment awareness can be fostered by intentional practice, or you can stop your self at any moment and use your senses to get out of your head and into life as it is now, as you are now. Self-awareness opens the door to change. Being in the present moment helps to open that door.

—

In this moment, use one of your senses to be present now.

91

Codependency can involve all sorts of distorted thoughts.

Becoming aware of what is going on in your mind is essential to self-recovery. Noticing when you are lost in thought is a good first step. The next step is to notice what you are thinking—both its content and its accuracy.

Noticing the content of your thoughts tells you where you are living your life. Is it your life or someone else's? Are your thoughts about someone else occasional or obsessive? Are they compulsive—out of your control? Obsessive thinking can be a driver of codependency.

Noticing the accuracy of your thoughts is also important. Thoughts are not always accurate or rational. Psychology calls these types of thoughts *cognitive distortions*. Cognitive distortions include all-or-nothing thinking, catastrophizing, minimizing, jumping to conclusions, discounting the positive, and personalizing. With codependency, some such thoughts may be *It's all my fault. I am unlovable. They said I did a good job, but they were just being nice. If I don't loan them the money, they will never speak to me again. If I have to leave early, they won't invite me again. If I say what I think, they will leave.*

Codependency is encouraged by such errors in thinking. As you can see from these examples, cognitive distortions can stop you from speaking up for your self, keep you from believing in your strengths, and generally be obstacles to change. Cognitive distortions keep you stuck, both in your usual mental loops and in the codependent behaviors that you carry too far.

—

In this moment, close this book and spend a few minutes noticing your thoughts. Just notice.

92

Catching errors in your thinking can be pretty cool.

Imagine freeing your self by changing your thinking! It can be done. For example, let's say you often tell your self, *I can't do this.* As you learn more about you, you decide instead to say, *With some effort, I can do that.* What a different message to your self! Your usual message is an all-or-nothing statement: can do / can't do. It leaves no gray area. The alternative statement moves out of all-or-nothing thinking and creates the possibility of change.

You may then be confronted with the next self-message: *I don't have it in me to make the effort.* Once again, you can visit that thought and decide if it is true or if you might think instead, *I can take small steps that I can handle. This doesn't have to be a gigantic effort all at once, right here and now!*

Freeing your self from thoughts that encourage your codependency include learning to tell your self: *It is okay for me to do something for myself. It is important for me to say what I need and want. I can give them half of the money they asked for. It is fine for me to join them for an hour and then go rest.*

Catching the errors in your thinking enables you to change your thoughts in the direction of accurate and realistic. Instead of being extreme and absolute, you can create honest and reasonable thoughts that give you space to do things differently. Pretty cool.

—

In this moment, identify an all-or-nothing thought of yours. If you can, create an alternative thought between all or nothing that is accurate and true for you.

93

Being realistic can free you to move forward.

We are more unrealistic than we believe ourselves to be. Think of how often you underestimate the amount of time it will take to get something done or overestimate what you can expect from someone else. We tell ourselves stories to justify our choices and actions and to sustain our hopes and dreams.

We also ignore certain stories to protect ourselves from the realities of our lives. We don't think about something that happened, we deny that it happened, or we believe it won't happen again—all to keep ourselves from feeling bad and hopeless.

Unrealistic thinking protects you. It also keeps you from growing. When you use unrealistic thoughts for decision-making and relationship-building, you remain stuck in your patterns of how you relate to others and treat your self. Though it can be a challenge, learning to accurately see and accept what *is* can free you to make valuable changes.

Instead of thinking *They can't do this without me*, a more realistic statement to self is *They can do this without me.*

Instead of thinking *If I say it enough times, they will get it*, a more realistic statement to self is *My repeating myself will not make things better.*

Instead of thinking *I only want what's best for them*, a more realistic statement to self is *I really don't know what is best for them.*

Do you find some of these realistic statements unsettling? That's okay. Being realistic is a big change that may upset you at first, but it can free you going forward.

—

In this moment, think of one unrealistic belief of yours.

94

Separating what is yours and not yours is self-recovery in action.

When you lose your self in someone else, it is difficult to separate you from them. You may be enmeshed in a number of ways—mentally, physically, and emotionally.

The following exercise will help you mentally separate you from your enmeshed relationship.

Imagine a line down the center of a page. You are on one side of the line. On the other side is the person you are involved with. The line is not a wall. It is simply where you end and the other person begins.

Now, think of a current problem or situation with this person. On your side of the line, list your responsibilities, feelings, and actions relative to the issue. As you stumble upon items for the other person—their responsibilities, feelings, and actions—put those items on their side of the line. This exercise increases self-awareness and brings clarity to the cloudiness of an enmeshed relationship.

You can also use this exercise to reinforce this clarity of mine/yours in this way. As you interact with the other person, you can take anything to the line: a statement, gift, request, or idea. Then, step back, leaving what you have offered and giving them space to consider what you have placed there. Be careful not to push you or your offering further on their side of the line. Respect them and stay steady with you. Your offering is theirs to do with as they choose.

—

In this moment, are you in a relationship situation that would benefit from your awareness of what is yours and what is not?

95

Leave it to the other person if it's theirs to do.

Probably sometime as a child you were told, "That's not yours." Whether you had taken something that belonged to a sibling or were reluctant to give back a toy to a friend, you were told what you had in your hands was not yours. It probably had a sting at the time, but the message was an important one: You can't go around making other people's things your own.

This not-yours message can be helpful to codependent people in recovery. We have good ideas. We see solutions. We can readily take a situation or problem out of someone else's hands and make it our own. Sometimes this serves a legitimate purpose, but not in *all* situations.

When you take time to separate what is yours and what belongs to the other person, this brings the awareness you need to decide what you should do. For those things on the other person's list—their responsibilities, feelings, or behaviors—unless it is a life and death emergency, it is best to leave them for the other person to take care of. They need to think for themselves, make their own arrangements, or speak up. The more you do for them, the less they can grow. They remain dependent on you, and you remain frustrated with their dependence even as you continue to take care of things that are theirs to do.

If it's someone else's, leave it to them and take care of what is yours. This is a balanced, fair, and adult-to-adult way of being that can benefit all.

—

In this moment, identify one thing that is not yours to do for someone you care about and imagine leaving it to them to be responsible for.

96

Work on the things on your side of the line.

The exciting thing about separating what is yours and not yours is that you can focus more on you! As you leave it to the other person to take care of what is theirs, you not only foster their growth but also set your stage for your growth.

So take a good look at what is on your side of the line, in your lane, in your yard. This may not be pleasing as you begin. In fact, you may have subconsciously been avoiding your list by focusing on others. Now you have your feelings, responsibilities, and behaviors more clearly in front of you. And since you are not as busy with the other person's list, you have some time for yours.

With curiosity and openness, let what is on your list seep in. Don't try to remedy or take action yet. Simply be with these pieces of you that you have identified. How do you feel? What is it you want for you? How do you spend your time? How would you like to spend your time? What are your responsibilities? What is important to you?

As you take this in, you may well find that some idea or action naturally emerges from your increased self-awareness—perhaps a call to a dear friend, a walk by yourself, a return to a hobby, a new class, or creating a space of your own in your home. Your ideas for you could be inspired and endless and very good for you.

—

In this moment, make a list of three things that are distinctly yours to notice and attend to.

97

Detaching means stepping back enough to see and think clearly.

When you are really upset, you are not in touch with your thoughts. You are in a reactive mode ready to take action—fight, flight, fawn, fix, or freeze. It is not physiologically possible to have your survival modes activated and think clearly. When danger is present, or you sense that it is, your neurobiological wiring prioritizes self-protection: *No time for thought. Act now!*

This is where detaching comes in. Healthy detaching is about finding balance in your thoughts and emotions, not letting them become so extreme that your body sets off its survival alarms. Detaching in this sense is not about leaving or ending a relationship. It is about becoming calm, centered, and able to think so you can make better decisions.

Detaching is stepping back from what is going on. You may literally step back, or you may only be able to step back your thoughts and emotions. Either way, the first step is to calm and center your self. Notice when your alarms are going off. Then, in a safe place, pause and reconnect with your breath and body. Tune into your feelings, needs, and wants. Take as much time as you need to honestly know what is true for you.

This stepping back of detaching is like moving a book away from your face so you can see the words clearly. Your eyes have to adjust. So it is as you step back and re-center in a tangled situation, giving your self space to see and think more clearly.

—

In this moment, literally step back from something so you can see it more clearly or fully. Take in this experience.

98

Listen as though you are watching a show.

Detaching is about stepping back from a situation so you can recover your thinking and emotional control. After you have calmed your self by consciously connecting with your breath and body sensations, shift into an observing stance—observing you, the other person, and the situation.

To settle into this observing mode, you might say to your self, *Just listen. Stay calm. Observe. Think. Take your time. Release tension. Breathe. Stay with self.* Each of these reminders helps you stay steady with your connection with you. Each gentle prompt supports the solid foundation you are building for you to stand on, a foundation not to tear down others but to build you up.

Having internally established your observational stance, take in what the other person is saying and doing as though they were on a stage or television. Just listen and notice. Take in what you are thinking and feeling and how your body is reacting to what is going on. Just listen and notice. Quiet your tendency to judge, and bring in patience and objectivity. Check in with your motivations in the situation. What are you trying to accomplish here? What is the other person trying to accomplish?

The more accurately and fully you observe what is happening in your interaction, the better able you will be to decide what to say or do—and the fewer regrets you will have about how you might have acted or spoken. Phew!

—

In this moment, think of a recent interaction that bothered you. Can you take an observer's stance and see and hear the other person more clearly? Can you see and hear you more clearly?

99

Respond rather than react.

When your defenses are up, it is easy to blurt out mean things, issue ultimatums you do not mean, or break off a relationship prematurely. We all say regrettable things when we are upset. We act in atypical and unbecoming ways and then carry guilt around with us for days thereafter. Nothing is gained—and in fact, something was likely lost—by our reactions.

Remember, reactions are your survival instincts stepping in to protect your upsetness. They serve important protective services, but their strength and speed can have you saying and doing things you have not thought through completely. You may not be fairly representing your self.

Responding means you deliver a message, answer, or plan that is true for you in a non-defensive manner. As you calm your self and observe the situation, you will be able to formulate thoughts and sentences and speak in an assertive (but not aggressive) tone to the other person.

Meeting an attack with an attack won't help. Defensiveness breeds defensiveness. Statements that begin with "you" inevitably set off defensiveness. Statements that begin with "I" are grounded and inarguable. They are about you—what you feel, think, need, or want. Find them within. Take your time. Figure them out. Then speak or act clearly, honestly, reasonably, and respectfully.

—

In this moment, think of a situation in which you reacted recently. In the calm and safety of now, listen to your self and construct an "I" statement that would have represented your self better then. What was true for you?

100

Talking to your self is a great idea.

You have probably heard that something must be wrong with you if you talk to your self. Well, self-recovery encourages you to talk to your self. As you pause and connect with you, self-talk can be quite useful in a number of ways.

Self-talk is an established technique in counseling. Self-talk includes reminders, affirmations, reassurances, or simply restating to self what you know is accurate in that moment. For example, *I am okay. It is okay to say this. I haven't done anything wrong. This is not my issue. I am not the problem. I don't want to become the problem.*

With codependency, you can be so pulled off your center as you interact with someone else that you become confused, frustrated, or lost. Self-talk helps you stay connected to the clarity you find when you pause, observe, and identify your "I" statement. Intentional internal conversations can anchor you in your assertive "I" statement.

Please make your internal conversations dialogues, not monologues. An internal monologue can take you right back to your usual thoughts and behaviors; it's the dialogue within you that helps you respond to your usual messages with your new self-understanding and self-awareness. As you talk with someone else, simultaneously have your own internal conversation—a real back-and-forth with you. This will help you stay clear and represent your self fairly.

—

In this moment, practice having an internal dialogue with your self about the next thing you plan to do today. Try not to let the monologue of "I'll do it later" or "There's no point in doing that" set in. Instead, aim for a real back-and-forth with your self.

101

Perhaps it's time to meet your emotions.

Self-awareness also involves awareness of your emotions. We all have feelings most of the time. Sometimes we are aware of them. Often, though, they are just outside our awareness. Sometimes we feel them in our body but push them away or say, "I shouldn't feel that way." Sometimes they are bothersome or scary, and we have no idea what to do with them or fear getting stuck in that powerful emotion. Sometimes they are positive or hopeful, and we don't let them in either.

Feelings are waiting for you to notice them so you can understand them/you and respond to them/you. When you feel ready, notice how your body is feeling, what your thoughts are telling you, and what emotions are arising here and now. Simply acknowledge your emotions one by one and hold them as you breathe deeply. Do your body sensations help you understand your emotions? Do your thoughts match and possibly encourage your emotions, whatever they may be? Is your emotion familiar to you? Does it make sense that you feel this way? You are becoming emotionally aware.

Now see if you can be more specific about your present emotions. For example, if you recognize the emotion as sad, does that mean you are disappointed or hopeless? If you are happy, do you feel calm or encouraged? Dig deeper so you can accurately identify your emotions and offer them the care they are asking of you.

—

In this moment, if you wish, close this book and bring your present emotions into your awareness. See how specifically you can name them.

102

Emotional care can be a lovely thing.

We talk about handling, managing, or regulating our emotions. All those words are accurate and useful. But how about we *care* for our emotions? Just as you receive medical care, you can give your self emotional care.

Your emotions are parts of you. They are not rascals there to pester or discourage you. If you see them as parts of you with important messages for you, you can develop a relationship with them. You can understand what they are telling you, and together you can figure out what you need.

When you care for something—like a plant, for example—you remember it is there. You give it your attention, providing it with water and fertilizer. You place it where it will get the right amount of light and warmth for its best growth. You do whatever you can for your plant to grow and thrive. This is care in action.

Offering your emotions this same level of attention and action supports your growth. Emotions ignored can make you sick. Emotions pushed aside rear their unhappy heads when you least expect it. Emotions you minimize or discount don't get to deliver the signals they are sending.

Caring for your emotions, on the other hand, can be a lovely thing. You can notice them, listen to them, and offer them the care they need right then and there.

—

In this moment, see if you can notice one particular emotion and listen to what care it would like from you.

103

Here is a menu of ways to care for your emotions.

You have choices about how to care for your emotions. Instead of feeling overwhelmed or scared by them, you can pay attention to them and then respond to them in the ways that are most fitting at the time. Here is a menu of ideas for emotional care.

- **Be with your emotions**. Tenderly hold your feelings as a parent would hold their child. As you calm you, your feeling is calmed, and you can look deeper into your feeling.
- **See your emotions as cues or signals.** What are they telling you that you need? Are you tired? Rest. Are you discouraged? Find comfort and support. Are you confused? Be still.
- **Contain your emotions**. Sometimes we don't know what to do with strong emotions. Emotional containment involves finding a way, a place, or a process to set down your emotions until you wish to pick them up again.
- **Communicate your emotions to someone**. You may first want to talk with a safe person about your emotions. Then, if you choose, you can communicate your emotions to the person they involve.
- **Change your neural structure** by letting the good seep in. Pleasant emotions—for example, when you receive a compliment or positive feedback—can profoundly help if you spend at least 30 seconds absorbing them. This absorption changes your brain structure toward positivity and emotional balance.

One emotional care strategy is not better than another. As you become familiar with this menu, you will know which strategy feels most helpful for you at a particular time or in a particular situation.

—

In this moment, study this emotional care menu.

104

Spiritual awareness can be a source of comfort and release.

Spirituality, the fourth area of self, means different things to different people. In self-recovery, we speak of spirituality as something beyond self. Some people have religious beliefs as their spiritual sources. Others find spiritually in nature, friendships, silence, the universe, or a time of day. Others do not subscribe to spirituality at all.

Any of these choices are okay. They are your choices. Your self-recovery journey is always about finding out what is true for you.

One way spirituality can be helpful to self-recovery is that it is readily accessible. In your calm presence, there is space for connecting not only with your body, thoughts, and emotions but also with something beyond your self, something intangible but possible and powerful. There are things you can't explain—lots of them. There are things not in your control—lots of them. What would it be like to let go of grasping for things not in your reach? Spirituality can help with this.

Spirituality is about establishing a relationship with your spiritual source. It is a relationship you come to know and trust. Your spiritual source receives your questions with patience and presence. It provides loving guidance to enrich and stabilize your life. It offers a calming presence, a safe relationship, something constant, reliable, and wise—something to call upon and to which you can hand over things not in your control.

—

In this moment, notice how you are responding to the idea of spirituality as an area of self that can help with your self-recovery.

105

Your spirituality is up to you.

You are invited to explore you and spirituality. Perhaps you have an active spiritual life that supports and guides you. Perhaps you don't believe in spirituality. Or perhaps you are somewhere between these two experiences. Wherever you may be, here are some questions to raise your awareness of you and this fourth area of self:

- Is spirituality a part of your life? If yes, in what ways are you spiritual? How does it show up in your life? If not, how are you feeling about this topic of spirituality?
- How do you make contact with your spirituality? How often and under what circumstances? Do you forget about your spirituality as a resource as you forge ahead?
- Is spirituality important to you? Does it make a difference in your life?
- Would you like to be more connected with your spiritual sources? How would you do that? How might that help you?
- How do you feel about including spirituality in your self-recovery? Does it have a place? Could it help?

Codependency recovery teaches us to let go of many things: trying to make things happen, change someone else, or control what is impossible for us to control. This sounds heavy, and it is. It is also freeing. Spirituality helps with letting go. It provides a source to which you release what is not yours. It supports you as you move forward with new understandings and faith that you are going in the right direction, even if the path is crooked at times.

—

In this moment, reread each of the above questions, taking a long pause between each one to see what answers come into your awareness.

Readings on

Self-Competence with Confidence

Self-competence is about learning new skills to support your growth.

As you grow in self-understanding and self-awareness, you may identify changes you want for you but not quite know how to make them happen. For example, you may want to not feel so guilty, to assert your self, or to set boundaries. This is where self-competence, the third element of self-recovery, comes in.

Self-competence is about developing skills that support your shift from your strong external focus to your attentive, responsive internal focus. Being competent means you have the necessary ability, knowledge, and skill to do something successfully. These readings on self-competence are designed to help you do just that—successfully develop your connection with you.

You can have improved self-understanding and self-awareness, but the nuts and bolts of healing shame and managing guilt need to be taught. Shame and guilt can run deep and may benefit from counseling, but you can also lessen the power of these emotions by learning some concrete skills. Assertiveness, too, needs to be taught. Simply being told to be assertive does not convey how to do that, nor does being told to "just say no." Saying no and setting other such boundaries takes knowledge and skill.

You probably have never been taught these skills. Few people have. Schools and social organizations typically don't teach these things, and most of us did not have these skills modeled successfully by our family of origin. Fortunately, it's never too late to learn some new skills that help you feel competent and confident. Ready?

—

In this moment, consider the skill sets mentioned above. Is there one in particular you are eager to learn more about?

107

As your confidence grows, so does your sense of self.

Self-competence builds self-confidence, which builds a sense of self. These building blocks are worthy of a careful look.

Self-competence is about developing skills that help you succeed in whatever you are doing. As your competence increases, so does your confidence. Think of reading. Most of us hardly remember when we first learned to read. Word by word, sentence by sentence, we developed our ability to read something and understand it. Paragraph by paragraph, chapter by chapter, our abilities improved until we felt confident about ourselves as readers.

This same pattern is true with learning a sport, playing a musical instrument, or becoming a good cook. Slow, deliberate initial steps repeated many times develop competence, which increases our confidence that we can throw a ball, play a tune, or cook a tasty meal.

Confidence definitely builds your sense of self. *Sense of self* refers to your understanding and acceptance of who you are. This involves knowing and respecting your values, beliefs, and feelings about your self. All of self-recovery is about supporting your sense of self. Self-understanding and self-awareness are components of a strong sense of self. So is self-confidence.

Self-confidence means you believe in your abilities and worth even when you are challenged. Self-confidence is not arrogance or conceit. It is a deeply and lovingly held belief in you—in your abilities, choices, and who you are.

—

In this moment, think of something you learned to do that you now feel confident about. Notice what confidence feels like and how it affects your sense of self.

108

These five foundational skills set you up for success.

To use most skill sets, you need to calm and center your self first. Whether you are trying to set a boundary, speak assertively, or quiet your guilt, connecting with your self first establishes an important foundation for remembering and applying new skills. Here are five foundational skills to help you do just that:

- **Pausing and stopping.** Take a moment for your self by interrupting whatever you may be thinking or doing, and open up space within to connect with you.
- **Mindful breathing.** Notice your experience of air coming in and out of your body at your nostrils or your diaphragm. Follow your breath for five cycles, settling into calm.
- **Quieting thoughts.** Notice your thoughts, but don't join them. Simply redirect your focus back to your inhalations and exhalations.
- **Releasing body tension.** Scan your body for tightness or unnecessary holding. Breathe in and out of these areas, releasing the tension you may find there.
- **Coming to the present moment.** In addition to using your body and breath to come into the present moment, you can use your senses. Notice how food tastes, see the sky, or smell your coffee.

These foundational skills set the stage for your successful use of any new skills. As you clear your mind and calm your body, you can then apply the skills you will be learning. And the more you practice these foundational skills, the better you will be at remembering them and using them when the time is right.

—

In this moment, if you wish, close this book and spend five minutes practicing these foundational skills.

109

There is so much power in a pause.

Have you ever said something you regretted? Done something hurtful when you were upset? Ended a relationship or quit a job before you calmed down?

Most of us have probably done some of those things. We get upset and take action. We are hurt and fight back. We are overwhelmed and blow our fuse. The irony is that as you said and did those reactive things to protect your self in the moment, you probably made things worse for your self instead of better.

This is where the power of the pause comes in. Self-recovery is built around learning to pause. It is the first step in retrieving your self from whatever you may be losing your self in. By pausing, you can shift your gears from full speed ahead to stopping so you can pull out your internal map and see if you are headed in the direction you want to be traveling.

The pause gives you clarity and stability.

Clarity comes from calming down so you can think. The more upset you are, the less you can think rationally or make good decisions. A pause helps you restore your amazing thinking abilities. Then you can become clear about what you are experiencing and what to do about it.

Stability comes from having enough calm and clarity to know where you stand. You are able to respond, rather than react, and can sustain your connection with your self even if you are challenged yet again.

—

In this moment, pause before you move on to the next thing in your day.

110

Codependency is a self-protective response to shame.

Shame is feeling like you are broken or unworthy. Guilt is the feeling of having done something wrong, while shame is feeling that something is wrong with you.

Shame can come from your life experiences. Growing up, you may have been given the message that something was terribly wrong with you. You may have been told that you deserved the bad things that happened to you and didn't deserve the good things that came your way. You may have old wounds that cause you embarrassment. You may have had traumatic experiences that make you feel bad about your self even if you didn't do anything wrong.

Codependency can be a self-protective response to shame. Shame can cause you to carry your codependent behaviors too far. Shame makes it uncomfortable for you to go within and listen to you. Shame tells you that you don't deserve to have a relationship-with-self.

When shame has you believing you are broken, you don't expect much from anyone. You prefer to keep your focus on others. You believe you cannot fix your brokenness, so you put your energy into fixing others.

When shame has you feeling unworthy, you believe you are undeserving. You don't ask for help. You don't expect much from others, and you don't ask to be treated fairly. You do not prioritize your self.

Shame hides out. You may not even be aware of shame as a powerful undercurrent in your life. That's okay. Just take in this information and be open to how some of it may apply to you.

—

In this moment, notice how you are feeling about this topic of shame.

111

Healing shame is possible.

Shame is not a burden you have to keep carrying. You do not have to live under its weight and let it affect how you treat others and your self. You do not have to hide out with your shame and disconnect from others. You do not have to overdo any number of things to make up for what you experience as your inadequacies.

Healing is possible, and it begins with recognizing your shame, if it is there. Sometimes shame is a deeper feeling hidden by anger, embarrassment, or shyness. You may have to explore your emotions to see if shame may be an underlying emotion. To help you with this, here are some questions to consider.

Are you aware when you feel shame? Where do you feel shame in your body? What thoughts alert you to your shame? What specific feelings arise that let you know you feel shame? What do you do when you feel shame?

It can also be helpful to think about your sources of shame. Do you carry shaming messages you received from unhelpful or unkind people? Does your shame come from not being willing or able to meet the expectations of others? Do you not feel good about how others perceive you? Do you feel misperceived by others? Are you misperceiving your self?

As you consider these questions, please be compassionate with your self. You are doing amazing work as you gently pry open this part of your self that has been locked away. Once opened, you can then greet your shame and continue together on your healing journey.

—

In this moment, if you wish, spend some time with these questions about you and shame.

112

Speaking with a safe someone about your shame can help to transform it.

As you journey on with healing your shame, you will do well to speak about it with someone who is safe for you. Remember, shame likes to live in the shadows where it festers and disturbs. It disconnects you from healthy relationships and keeps fear alive. When you reach out to a safe someone, your shame is met with empathy and understanding, and it loses its destructive power.

First, you have to be willing to reach out to someone to talk about your shame. Willingness is an essential ingredient of change that comes from within. Reaching out may be scary for you. Shame itself makes reaching out difficult, and often codependency adds to your reluctance to ask for help.

Remember that safe others are people who understand you and support your self-recovery work. They believe in you, wish you well, and will not make you sorry that you told them something.

When you are ready, you can talk with this safe person about your experiences with shame and what you understand about it. If you are speaking with a person who is fully present and engaged with you, you will feel their empathy. Empathy means they genuinely understand your story and emotions. This empathy builds connection, which helps you realize you are not alone or broken. As you experience this, your shame transforms into feeling accepted, affirmed, and of value—feelings to openly receive and deeply absorb.

—

In this moment, can you think of a safe someone to share your dark, burdensome secrets with?

113

When you are ready, releasing your shame lightens you and lights your path forward.

As you heal your shame, releasing its remnants can give additional healing. To discourage old issues from reigniting, creating a letting-go strategy can further unburden you of shame.

Before releasing your shame, make sure you are healing from it. You are not trying to shoo it away before you have given it the attention it needs. That would be yet another way of hiding your shame. Recognize and understand your shame, and speak with a safe someone about it. As you heal, you can feel compassion and connection, not fear and disconnection.

Releasing is different from hiding. When you hide something, it is still there, whether it can be seen or not. When you release something, it is no longer active in your life. You remember it, but your head and heart don't dwell on it. It does not affect you daily. Here are some ideas for releasing when you are ready:

- Write down on paper what you want to release. Then, burn the paper, dissolve it, tear it up, or put it in a public mailbox with no address.
- In your mind's eye, take the harmful messages you received from other people and give them back to them.
- Say to your self, *Not mine. Not true.*
- Entrust what you are releasing to your spiritual source.
- Release through your exhalations.
- Let go in an imagined or physical way to the wind, fire, air, or water.

—

In this moment, identify something you feel ready to release and try one of these letting-go ideas or one of your own.

114

Guilt loves to step in.

You may notice that, as you start knowing your self better and finding your voice, guilt steps in. As you think of taking an hour for yourself, you may think, *Yes, but I would feel guilty about that.* As you imagine saying no to something you don't have time for, you may think, *I would feel too guilty if I said that.* Guilt can stop you from doing exactly what you want or saying exactly what you mean. Guilt can easily overpower other thoughts and feelings, keeping you stuck in your patterns of overfunctioning for others and underfunctioning for self.

Guilt comes when you feel like you have done something wrong. Sometimes we *have* done something wrong—perhaps we forgot something or we failed to do what we said we would do. This is *merited guilt.* In these situations, feeling guilty is understandable and is an opportunity to fix whatever has been wronged.

Often, though, codependent people feel *unmerited guilt* when we have *not* done anything wrong—for example, when you:

- Say no to someone
- Believe you have disappointed or displeased someone
- Have needs and preferences that are different from others'
- Take time for your self
- Receive help from someone

Your self-recovery work will help you work with your guilty parts so you don't lose your self in your guilt but instead have more space within to listen and respond authentically to you.

—

In this moment, think about you and guilt. Do you experience guilt when you do something for your self?

115

Don't let your guilt take over.

Guilt can be like a loud child (or adult) insisting on having their way. Guilt can be dominant, powerful, and persistent. Your guilt is specific to you—it is a part of you trying to tell you something. Listen to what your guilt is saying. Your guilt can be protecting you from your fear of change, worry about what others think, or uncomfortableness with doing something different.

Getting to know your guilty parts is one way to manage your guilt. You can also use the following ideas to help you have a complete and accurate picture of you rather than being overpowered by your guilt:

- Recognize what you have done for the person or situation you are concerned about (rather than focusing on what you have not done). Make a mental list of time you have spent with them or things you have done for them. The list, which is only for you, is to help you get a balanced perspective as you say no or do less.
- Appreciate what you have done. Absorb your list, taking time to honestly recognize and value what you have done.
- You can also notice other feelings you may be having in addition to guilt. Guilt can be so strong that it drowns out your awareness of other emotions going on at the same time, about the same thing. Your other emotions can counterbalance the power of guilt and tell you more about the choices you are making for you.

—

In this moment, would you like to not let guilt have its way when you haven't done anything wrong?

116

Re-minding yourself of why you said or did something can help center you once again.

Many times, as soon as we deliver our "no," guilt moves in. Too often, we join our guilt rather than stay with our "no." We may think, *Oh, never mind. I can do what I want to do later.* Or *Well, maybe I can do what they asked of me. That was selfish of me to turn them down.*

A helpful thing to do in this moment of retreating from your choice is to remember your reasons for your decision. Remember why you said no. Remember why you don't want to be with that person. Remember why you won't loan money again. Guilt makes it difficult to remember your reasons. The further you get from your original decision, the more power guilt can have.

That's why it is important to re-mind your self of your reasons. *Re-minding* means resetting your thinking, sometimes again and again. As your guilt settles in, your thinking loses its clarity and accuracy. Instead of being realistic, your unsupported hopefulness about the other person surfaces. Instead of being fair and balanced, your focus on the other person dominates once again. Re-minding is an active way to help you stay your course.

And in the spirit of re-minding, re-mind your self that it is okay and important to take care of you. Guilt diminishes and distorts this message. It's up to you to kindly re-mind your self that you are a valuable person with your own needs, ideas, and plans worthy of equal consideration.

—

In this moment, take in this idea of re-minding.
It can help you stay connected with you.

117

You can develop your assertive voice.

Has anyone ever suggested that you be assertive? Did you know what that meant? Perhaps you thought it meant to stand tall and speak loudly or give someone a piece of your mind. Well, this is where skills come in. Most of us are not born knowing how to be assertive, nor was it modeled for us. But you can learn to be assertive, and it will make a positive difference in your life.

Being assertive means that as you speak for your self, you are aware of your emotions, keep them under your control, and act respectfully toward both you and the other person. An easy way to think about assertiveness is to put it on a continuum of ways we express our self. At the left end of the continuum is *passive*; at the right end of the continuum is *aggressive*. *Assertive* lies in the middle range.

We all travel along this continuum. We can start out in the assertive zone, get ramped up, and end up in the aggressive zone. We can start out passive and then, when we've had more than enough, we bolt to the aggressive end, skipping assertive completely.

You can learn how to stay in the assertive zone. You can learn to stay connected with what you want to say and how you want to say it. Just as you may have learned to parallel park between two cars, you can learn to navigate your self so that you are positioned in the assertive zone where you are safe, solid, and clear with your self and others.

—

In this moment, take in the image of the continuum of passive, assertive, and aggressive.

118

Upsetting someone would be upsetting.

Assertiveness lies between passivity and aggressiveness. Let's look at passivity. In general, being passive is saying or doing nothing. Letting something slide. Pretending like nothing happened.

When you consider codependency and passivity, there are some specific things going on that keep us in the passive zone. Because we can be so focused on others, we may not know what we think or feel, so we have nothing to say. We are blank and not engaged.

Or we may have some things we would like to express, but we do not trust our self. We tell our self that we don't know what we are talking about or that no one wants to hear from us.

Or we are afraid that if we do speak up, we will upset someone. They may get mad or feel hurt. There may be disagreement or conflict. The reactions of others scare us and keep us silent. So, we go along with something we disagree with or hide away hoping no one will find us and try to continue the conversation we want to avoid.

Upsetting others upsets us, too. It can upset us so much that it's hard to think and makes us regret ever saying one word. But not speaking up can be problematic in the long run. Frustration and impatience build and we explode in some way, abruptly jumping into aggression. Now we have the conflict and upset we were avoiding, times ten.

There must be something in the middle. There is. It's called assertiveness.

—

In this moment, can you identify some of the ways you can be passive?

119

Trying to make a point can be pointless.

Assertiveness lies between passivity and aggressiveness. Let's look at aggression. In general, being aggressive can include accusing, blaming, or demeaning. It is pointing the finger at the other person with a clear "you" message. Aggression can move from words to physical actions like throwing things, pushing, or hitting. With aggressive behavior, you are not in control of your emotions and are not respectful of you or the other person.

When you consider codependency and aggression, there are some specific yet subtle ways that our aggression may show up. Because we may have a strong need to be in control, we become attached to making our point to someone else. We repeat ourselves. We try different ways to explain what we mean. We want to convince the other person to join our point of view. As we hammer away at trying to get them to see or do something we want, we become more forceful. Usually, this leads to an argument, not understanding. Our overstating is pointless.

Codependent people can believe we are right. Sometimes we are, but what we think is right for us is not necessarily right for the other person. As we insist on being right, we fall into the hole of arguing and fighting. Notice the aggression. Righteous back-and-forth can dig a pretty big hole that's hard to get out of.

There must be something in the middle. There is. It's called assertiveness.

—

In this moment, can you identify some of the ways you can be aggressive?

120

"I" statements provide solid ground to stand on.

When we are assertive, we speak for our self. We have thought ahead, we know what is true for us, and we express it by starting our sentence with "I." For example, "I don't want to do that now." "I can help you on Saturday." Being clear about your "I" statement is an excellent setup for clear communication. It is solid ground. Sometimes it takes time and effort to figure out your "I" statement, but it is there waiting for you to put it together.

As you express your "I" statement, you do not have to defend or overexplain it. It is perfectly okay to have your own thoughts, feelings, and needs. In fact, it is more than okay—it is normal. If someone pushes back on your "I" statement, be ready to speak like a broken record with clear and committed repetitions of your "I" statement made in a neutral tone of voice.

Pay attention to any temptations to move from your assertiveness to passivity or aggression; watch for your usual ways of being passive or aggressive. Re-anchor in your "I" statement as often as needed to stay steady in the zone of assertiveness.

Assertiveness is not necessarily easy, but it is worth the effort. Developing your assertive voice involves clarity of thought, emotional control, and mutual respect. With those strong pieces of self-recovery in place, you can respond, rather than react in any given situation as you feel the solid ground under you and strength within.

—

In this moment, can you formulate an "I" statement to respond to something going on in your life now?

121

What exactly are boundaries?

Setting boundaries means defining the limits of what you will and won't accept in a particular situation or with a specific person. It does not mean building walls that cut you off from others or attaching your self to rules that don't work in all situations. Setting heathy boundaries is about listening to you, figuring out your limits, and asserting them to you and the people involved.

Boundary setting is important to your recovery from codependency. Many codependent people say they are not good at setting boundaries. Either we don't set them or we back down from a boundary we set. No blame—this is just our challenge. We believe, *If I say no, they won't call me again. If I say I won't pay for that, they will be mad at me.* Because of our internal conflicts and habitual patterns, setting boundaries requires specific skills.

Don't rush into setting your boundaries. It is too easy to be reactive and say things you don't really mean. That's when you give in and even apologize, leaving the core issue unresolved once again. Instead, take time to figure out your boundary and be ready to stick with it as you say it and live with it.

And remind your self that setting boundaries is a healthy thing to do. It can feel unkind, but in fact you are defining what is and is not okay for you in your relationships. Children need boundaries; so do the adults with whom we interact. And we certainly need to set limits with our self, too.

—

In this moment, kindly assess how you are at setting boundaries.

122

Begin setting a boundary by listening to you.

Boundary setting begins with you. Step aside and check in with you so you can create a boundary you have in your control and can live with.

Begin by slowing down. Pause, breathe, take a break, and connect with you. Listen to your four areas of self: body, mind, emotions, and spirit. Each area has valuable information about the boundary that is right for you. Your mind may be telling you one thing and your body may be giving you a different message. Listen with respect to each area and consider all their messages as you figure out your most genuine "I" statement.

This should be a statement, not a question. Questions are tentative and invite discussion: "Would it be okay with you if I ______?" A statement has strength and clarity: "I have decided that I will not be able to ______." Study and edit your "I" statement, making sure it is what you mean and something you can and will live with. Threats do not promote clean, clear relationships. Then, rehearse your boundary. Say it out loud to your self and to someone who is supporting you in your growth.

All of this is work to be done before you say anything to the other person. It is spending time with you so you can figure out what you want to say or do that respects your time, energy, body, and soul.

—

In this moment, is there a boundary you would like to set with your self or someone else? If so, see if you can create an "I" statement using these ideas.

123

How you express your boundary makes a world of difference.

Once you have figured out your genuine "I" statement and rehearsed it, the next step is to express your boundary to the people it involves. Your goals are to stay connected with you and your well-discerned boundary as you deliver it. Here are some ideas to help you with that:

- **Be assertive.** Stay close to your "I" statement and be ready to repeat it as necessary when you feel challenged or start to doubt your self. Speak in a neutral, informing tone.
- **Be prepared to stick with your boundary.** Stay connected with your commitment to the boundary you carefully crafted for you. Letting go of your boundary suggests you don't really mean it.
- **Don't overexplain your reasons.** Codependent people can feel like we have to justify most things, and in so doing, we elaborate too much. Overexplaining opens the door to further conversations and negotiations, which can dilute the strength and clarity of your "I" statement. The less said, the stronger your message and your self-connection. All you need to say is in your "I" statement. Imagine that!
- **Stick with the identified topic.** Stay focused on your "I" statement and the specific situation it is addressing. When you feel drawn toward bringing in old issues and complaints, redirect you back to the boundary you are setting for this particular person in this particular situation.
- **Stay in the present.** Use awareness of your breath and body to anchor you.

—

In this moment, review these ideas and identify at least one of them you want to remember and practice.

124

Be ready to live with the boundary you set.

Sometimes the bigger challenge is not the setting of the boundary but living with the changes it brings. Maybe that's one of the reasons setting boundaries is difficult—it involves change. A boundary can change how you spend your resources and how you engage with someone else. It can change your thoughts and feelings and help heal your body.

Living with your boundary is an inside job. It is up to you. Here are some ideas to help you along the way:

- **Connect with your strengths and belief in you.** Give your self messages of confidence and reassurance: *I know you can do this.* When we are upset, we lose track of our strengths, so reconnect with them and find more along the way.
- **Listen, but be careful not to overdefend or overexplain your choices.** Listen to what the other person has to say and let them know what you hear. At the same time, stay connected with you and your boundary. Don't try to get the other person to agree with you or be pleased with your boundary. Such efforts can entangle you all over again.
- **Know when to stop participating in a conversation about your boundary.** When you tune into your four areas of self as well as the tone and direction of the conversation, you know when it is time to stop talking.
- **Stop.** Simply say you have nothing else to say at this time and go somewhere else if needed.

—

In this moment, review these ideas and identify at least one of them you want to remember and practice.

125

Remember why you set your boundary.

As time goes by and emotions calm down, it is easy to let go of a boundary. We forget what prompted the boundary and why it was important to us then. For example, let's say that after much thought, you decided to end a relationship. Two weeks after you ended it, the two of you talk and decide to give the relationship another try. Two weeks after that, you realize you are once again living with the very things that made you end the relationship in the first place. You now remember why you ended the relationship.

Staying connected with your reasons for your boundary is super important to living with it. As hope or guilt slide in after boundary setting, your thinking softens and starts focusing on the consequences of your boundary. Fears and second-guessing are common. The more your thinking goes in this direction, the more you lose touch with the reasons for your boundary.

Remind your self of why you decided on your boundary. Reset your thinking so that as you live your post-boundary life, you are also connected with your "I" statement and the factors involved in your decision. Make a list of your reasons. Put up loving reminders. Pay attention to how you are feeling with your boundary in place. Talk with a safe someone who welcomes your reminders of why the boundary you set was necessary. And talk to your self, too, offering kindness, reassurance, and companionship.

—

In this moment, think of a boundary you recently set and remind your self of why you set it.

126

No.

You have probably heard this before: "No" is a complete sentence. That is true, but for codependent people, this sentence can stir up deeper issues that make it difficult to deliver a clean, solid "no."

We may be afraid that our "no" will displease someone, make them mad, or disappoint them. These are understandable concerns, to an extent. The problems come when our concern about the other person's reaction overrides our own feelings and needs. If pleasing someone else means you run out of money, that's a problem. If keeping someone from being mad means you are secretly mad, that's a problem.

At an even deeper level, we may be afraid that we will be abandoned if we stick with our "no." We believe we have to do exactly what the other person wants in order to keep our relationship. Or, we don't want to say no because we want things to be done the way we think they should be done. Saying no means leaving it to someone else, which can be unsettling if you like to control things.

Get to know your emotional parts that show up as you try to set your boundary so that you can ultimately commit to "no" when you mean it. And when you are ready to say no, remember to keep it simple: "No. I am not able to do that." No explanations needed. Notice when it is time to stop talking about your "no," and then stop. Let your thoughtfully delivered "no" speak for itself.

—

In this moment, is there a "no" you want to say to someone or to your self?

127

Yes.

"Yes" can be a fine answer. Boundaries are not all about saying no. They are about taking time to figure out what suits you. You may well want to say yes to something. You may relish the request. But first stop to make sure that you truly want to say yes and consider how your "yes" fits with your current life.

When we have not done this, we get in trouble with ourselves. We overload our plate without noticing whether we are already full or whether we want to leave room for dessert. But if you have run the boundary by you and you feel like you want to say yes, go for it!

Even with a yes, all the guidelines for boundary setting apply. Stick with the specific thing you are saying yes to, being careful not to add on additional yeses you haven't agreed to. Don't feel like you have to justify your "yes" to others or especially to your self. If worry or guilt about your "yes" creep in, reassure those emotional parts of why you have said yes and how it benefits you. This requires that you remember why you decided on "yes" in the first place. Stay close to your reasons for "yes" and take in what happens as a result of your "yes." There are lessons to learn from your choice. Maybe your plate was too full and you overestimated your capacity. Lesson learned. Maybe you feel wonderful being engaged in whatever you said yes to. Maybe it is just what you needed. Take that in. Lesson learned here, too.

—

In this moment, is there a "yes" you want to say to someone or to your self?

Readings on

Self-Attunement with Care

128

What is self-attunement?

The first three elements of self-recovery—self-understanding, self-awareness, and self-competence—are essential to your shift from focusing so much on others to focusing equally on you. Self-attunement is the fourth and final element of self-recovery. It completes the circle of four interlocking elements that hold and support your relationship-with-self in the center. Self-attunement solidifies and deepens this connection you are developing with you.

Self-attunement is about really tuning in to you. It builds from self-awareness and goes deeper. Think of tuning an instrument. When someone tunes a guitar, they listen carefully to the note and adjust the string in the smallest ways to arrive at the desired tone. This involves careful attention to the sounds and knowing what is needed to make a note clear, accurate, and beautiful.

Self-attunement is learning how to attune to your self in this same responsive way. Perhaps you were not attuned to as a child. Perhaps your caregivers did not stop and listen. Perhaps you did not feel heard or understood. Perhaps you still seek this attunement from others. That would be understandable.

Grieving what you did not get growing up is important. As you grow from your grief, a choice you have is to give your self the things you long for through self-attunement—sensitivity, responsiveness, consistency, warmth, comfort, security. As you attune to your body, mind, emotions, and spirit, you can make adjustments that make your connection with you clear, accurate, and beautiful.

—

In this moment, think of something you tune—an instrument, a radio dial, a balance scale, even the volume of something—and what that experience of tuning is like.

129

Self-attune with care.

Attuning to your self is a loving act to be done carefully. When attended to with focus and curiosity, self-attunement adds commitment, comfort, and security to your evolving relationship with you. This is the ultimate goal of self-recovery.

Self-attuning with care means being patient and attentive to your thoughts, feelings, choices, and actions. In the busy-ness of our lives, it's easy to not stop and notice what is going on with us—how we actually are in the moment. Without that internal information, we cannot make changes. We are on our personal autopilot.

Careful attuning is like you heard a noise in the night and are listening super carefully to figure out what that was. Careful attuning is the effort you make to hear what someone is saying to you in a noisy space, to zoom in and narrow your focus so you can accurately discern the messages coming your way.

Self-attune with care means to attune to your self with kindness, openness, and self-compassion. Judging your self adds weight to your self-recovery work—weight that not only slows you down, but can bring your growth efforts to a halt. As one person in self-recovery said, "I need to be empathetic with my self." Yes. Empathy goes a long way in feeling heard, understood, and accepted. You offer empathy to others; how about offering it to your self, too, as you carefully attune to you?

—

In this moment, see if you can attune to you with the same focus you might use to hear someone speaking to you from another room.

130

Self-attunement incorporates the elements that promote a secure attachment.

The word *attune* is often used in describing attachment styles. A secure attachment develops when the primary caregivers attune to their young child. They pay attention to the sounds, gestures, and facial expressions the child makes. They mirror and echo those communications back to the child, letting the child know that they see, hear, and perhaps understand them. This intimate communication reassures the child that their caregivers are with them. It validates the child's existence and value. The child sees the caregivers as a secure base from which to explore and master the world. This gives the child an internal security that promotes confidence, comfort, and the ability to grow.

Self-attunement is about offering your self this same level of attunement. It means letting go of your external agendas and instead being with you. It is the same type of attunement you might offer to your own child or to close friends and family who need you. In these cases, you stop and give them your full attention. You listen to their words, watch their expressions, feel their energy, notice their behaviors. All of this helps you to understand them and know how to respond.

This is the model for self-attunement. What we so freely and readily offer to others is what we are learning to offer to our self, as well. Listen to you—notice your feelings, behaviors, and gut reactions. Reassure your self that you exist and are of deep value. You are creating a secure base within as you reliably attune to you.

—

In this moment, reflect on how it feels when you know someone is really attuned to you.

131

Self-attunement involves further strengthening of your internal focus.

As you know, self-recovery is all about shifting from being so focused on people and things outside of you to being able to focus within you, as well. Self-recovery is about learning how to make that shift and experiencing the benefits of connecting with you throughout your day.

Self-attunement involves a deeper commitment to going within. *Deeper* in this case means more regular, more reliable, and more focused. It doesn't mean you must have a dedicated place, a cleared schedule, or a lot of time. It does mean you believe in your value and know that the health you seek involves tuning into you so you can recognize what you need and how to respond.

You are learning to access your self. You are learning how to go within and explore. You are learning how to notice your body, thoughts, emotions, and spirit in more detail. You will get to know your internal terrain—your wishes, hopes, values, patterns, and personality. As you internally explore, you will encounter challenges to going within, parts that show up protectively and make it difficult for you to be still and be with you. You will learn how to work with those parts and gain greater access to you. You will then find answers you did not know were there. You will be inspired in ways that surprise you. You will come to trust you and your recovery process.

All of this is possible when you self-attune with more intentional awareness, discernment, and care than ever before.

—

In this moment, how are you feeling about an even deeper commitment to connecting with you?

132

Each day, have intentional times to pause, connect, and check in with you.

One way to increase your internal focus is to have a time, at least once each day, when you intentionally stop and connect with you. It doesn't have to be a long time. Within five minutes you can make a noticeable shift to calm, centered, and self-attuned. Here is a simple exercise to guide you:

- **Pause** periodically throughout your day in a safe place. Let your hands be free and your posture comfortably upright.
- **Connect** with you by releasing tension in your body. Follow the natural cycle of your breath, focusing on your inhalations and exhalations—experiencing them, not thinking about them.
- **Notice** what is going on in your body, mind, emotions, and spirit. Check in on each of these areas without judgment. You are attuning to you. What messages is your body sending you? What are your thoughts and emotions? Are you connected with your spirit?
- **Reflect** on what you are becoming aware of through your attunement. Don't overthink it, but allow your self to make some mental notes about what you are noticing within. Maybe some great idea comes to you. Maybe you remember something important to you. Maybe you want to respond to some part of you that you are connecting with.
- **Respond** is something you choose to do at a later time based on what you are learning about you. In the meanwhile, complete this exercise by letting go of your noticing and reflecting and follow your diaphragmatic breath for several more cycles.

—

In this moment, give this self-attunement exercise a try.

133

Within you is your garden of self.

Metaphors are excellent teachers. They help us see things in a different light. They help us see what we have no idea we are not seeing. *Garden of self* is a rich metaphor for your self-recovery work. It highlights the planting and tending that both a garden and you require for healthy growth. Compassion, care, accurate thoughts, and intentions to pause and connect within are some of the many seeds you are sowing. Once planted, tending to those seeds is essential. Watering and fertilizing are necessary for growth. And so it is with your garden within.

There are all types of gardens. There are vegetable gardens, flower gardens, and rock gardens. Gardens can be in a window or in your backyard. They can be on an empty city lot or your patio. Gardens can be planted in the earth, fancy pots, or recycled cans. You get the point. Gardens are as different as people are. Each of us has a garden within that is of our own making and design, whether we are aware of that or not.

Self-recovery invites you to connect with your garden of self. What have you, the gardener, planted there? Is it what you want? How's your garden growing? What seems to help your garden be fruitful? What are you doing with those fruits of your talents and efforts?

—

In this moment, spend a few extra minutes considering the questions about your garden of self in the last paragraph.

134

What are you planting in your garden within?

Let's continue with the metaphor of your garden within. It has a number of important messages for you to consider as you grow from codependency into self-recovery.

Before we look at what you are planting in your garden, let's take a look at what has already been planted there over the years. Messages people have given you about you are there. Life experiences that made you feel particular ways are well established. Hopes that have or have not been actualized, dreams that have or have not come true, and the core way you see yourself are all growing in your garden. As you move toward consciously planting in your garden of self, you may have some weeding you want to do first.

Now, let's look at what you are planting in your internal garden these days. You have been spending time with these readings. Have any of them seemed like something good to plant within you? You have learned to pay attention to your body, thoughts, emotions, and spirit. Have you planted any seeds of daily awareness in these areas? You have been encouraged to offer kindness and consideration to your self, just as you offer them to others. Have you been able to plant compassion or nonjudgment in your garden? You have been learning to notice the messages you give to you about you. Have you planted some supportive self-talk that lovingly keeps you on your new track?

—

In this moment, what do you want to be planting in your garden of self? Take time to consciously consider this reading and its questions for you, the gardener.

135

Gardens need nurturing care.

Have you ever bought a healthy, happy plant and forgotten to take care of it? It may have been potted and only needed you to remember to water it. It may have needed to be repotted or put in the ground. You kept seeing it and promising to get around to tending to it. But you never did.

Most of us know what this neglect looks like. The worst outcome is that the plant died. Short of that, the plant struggled to thrive. Your past-due care of the plant may have saved it, but it took a long time to recover and grow once again.

Your garden within needs nurturing care, just like the plant you brought home. This is where the metaphor of the garden of self enriches your work. Not only do you, the gardener, want to consciously plant seeds in your garden, but you also need to foster their growth after you plant them. Nurturing your garden means to remember to water, fertilize, weed, and prune it to keep it growing strong.

In self-recovery, this nurturing includes pausing and connecting with you, offering self- supportive messages, learning more things to encourage your growth, talking with others on a similar path, and engaging in daily practices that keep you in touch with what you are growing in your garden of self.

And you certainly want to keep toxic chemicals out of your precious garden of self. You know what they do.

—

In this moment, how can you nurture the seeds you have planted in your garden of self?

136

Gardens need protection.

Nurturing your garden of self includes protecting it. Gardens with vegetables, fruits, and flowers are subject to the appetites of all sorts of creatures above and below ground. Deer, groundhogs, and moles eat entire plants. Birds, caterpillars, and insects nibble on the fruits and leaves. When you, the gardener, see that your plants are damaged or destroyed, it is quite discouraging.

Gardens can be protected in a number of ways, including netting, fences, and maybe a scarecrow or two. Each gardener takes specific steps to protect what they are growing. They cannot just walk away from their garden and hope that when they return sometime later, their plants will still be there and growing strong.

The same is true for you as you cultivate your garden within. If you have planted thoughtful seeds and tended them into sprouts, don't you want to protect them so they can grow big and strong? If you are working on being assertive, it is good to protect your self from someone who tells you don't know what you are talking about. If you are taking time each day to be still and listen to you, it is good to do that where you won't be interrupted or discounted. If you are excited about having some time alone, it is wise to protect that seedling from being uprooted by your guilt. Consciously create an invisible fence that only lets the good into your garden within—good from others and especially good from you.

—

In this moment, can you identify what you need to protect your garden of self from? What creatures lurk just outside of its edges?

137

Gardens have gates and gatekeepers.

Fences protect a garden, but you also need to be able to get into the garden. A gate makes that possible.

As with a physical garden, you will need a gate into your garden of self so you can tend to what you are growing there. You have been visualizing your garden within. Now imagine your gate into it. It may be wrought iron, wood, or wire. It may be simple or ornate.

What happens when you try to open your gate? Can it be easily opened? Do you struggle to get it open? Or is it locked? Gates themselves have devices to protect their use. Some gates require an alignment of parts in order for the gate to open. Other gates are locked and need a key or combination to get in.

The gate to your garden within may have such protectors, too. Let's call them your gatekeepers. Gatekeepers are parts of you that are protecting you. Many of them have been on the job for a long time. They are probably responsible for how well-used or stuck your gate into you may be. Sometimes they let you go within; sometimes they challenge your entrance.

You will want to befriend your gatekeepers so you can comfortably and productively be in your garden of self. You will learn more about how to do this in later readings. First, just know that your gatekeepers will likely meet you at your gate as you try to open it and go within. They are parts of your internal gardenscape, too.

—

In this moment, think of a gate you have encountered, maybe at a swimming pool, an entrance to the subway, or a toll booth. What was required of you to pass through that protective gate?

138

Your gatekeepers are protective parts of you.

Self-recovery is ultimately about developing your relationship-with-self. As you are learning, this involves getting to know your different parts as they show up. We all have a variety of parts and speak of them naturally when we say, "Part of me wants to do that, and part of me doesn't."

Gatekeepers are one such part. When you are going within, your gatekeepers show up protectively. In the past, it may not have been safe for you to have your own thoughts or feelings. You may have been discouraged from doing anything that seemed selfish. You may not have learned how to handle strong feelings or how to discern your own opinion, so why would you want to go within you, where you might be challenged to do these things?

To help you notice and identify your gatekeepers, let's name some of them:

- **Trauma responses,** including fight, flight, freeze, fawn, and fix
- **Characters,** such as child parts and adult parts
- **Emotions,** such as shame, guilt, fear, and regret
- **Thoughts,** such as *I am no good* or *I'm not worth caring about*
- **Behaviors,** such as staying busy or scrambling to keep the peace

Recognizing your gatekeepers and naming them will be quite helpful as you negotiate access to your garden within. Remember, these gatekeepers are protective. While they mean no harm, they may be working too hard to protect you in ways you no longer need.

—

In this moment, take in this list of gatekeepers. Are any of them showing up as you try to connect with you?

139

Meet and greet your gatekeepers.

We are not used to turning inward. So, as we begin to connect with self, the gatekeepers at the entrance to our garden of self say things like, "You don't have time for this! This is weird. I wouldn't go in there." Strong thoughts and feelings present themselves. Restless, distracting behaviors step in. These are all gatekeepers.

It is natural to try to chase these gatekeepers away or else to be intimidated and retreat to your usual ways of being. Your gatekeepers, though, are not trying to keep you out. They are protecting you and your internal garden. They want to keep you safe. Your garden would not have a gate with a keeper if the intention was to keep you completely disconnected from you. There would simply be a wall or fence with no entrance.

By cultivating a reasonable and responsive relationship with your gatekeepers, you can access self through a mutual, respectful relationship, like the relationship you would have with family, friends, and neighbors.

With this in mind, meet and greet your gatekeepers. Notice them and call them by name, if possible—for example, shame, guilt, or fear. Get to know them: What is their job? What are they protecting? What do they want you to know about them? Quiet your judgment and offer curiosity and patience. Imagine you are on a walk in your community and run into a neighbor who you don't know and who you have to walk by to get where you are going. How would you converse with them?

—

In this moment, imagine a conversation you might have as you greet a neighbor or friend you just ran into.

140

Let your gatekeepers get to know you.

As you get to know your gatekeepers, it will be helpful for your gatekeepers to get to know you. After you greet them and learn some things about them, tell them some things about you.

Explain why you want to go into your garden of self. They may be quite surprised to find you at their gate, since you have not come here often in the past. You might tell them about your desires to be less anxious, to have more internal peace, to know how to speak for yourself. You might talk about your self-recovery journey and what you ultimately want for you. Your gatekeepers may have questions for you. Answer their questions patiently and honestly. You are building a relationship.

As your internal conversations with your gatekeepers continue, ask them, "What would make you feel safe enough for me to enter my garden of self and spend time there?" Listen, and then, with the understanding you gain, offer appreciation, reassurance, and workability.

Thank your gatekeepers for all they do to keep you safe. Reassure them that you are not uprooting their long-standing role but wondering if they would like to take a break or change their job a bit. See if you can imagine a solution that you both feel comfortable with, a solution that honors what they do for you *and* lets you into your garden within. Maybe your visit will be short at first. Maybe your gatekeeper will travel with you into the garden just in case you need protection.

—

In this moment, what would you say to your gatekeepers about why you want to enter your garden within?

141

You are developing mutual, respectful relationships with your gatekeepers.

As the various parts of you learn to live together, you can develop an authentic relationship with your self. Instead of your internal parts pulling and tugging, helping and restricting, cheering and discouraging, they listen to each other and work things out with your guidance. That guidance comes from your adult parts—your insights, your strengths, your allies. These parts have wisdom and maturity you can utilize to foster your internal community. And the more harmonious that community, the greater your capacity for self-attunement—for deeper and fuller awareness of your body, mind, emotions, and spirit.

Developing a relationship with each gatekeeper is an ongoing process that is best approached with respect and mutuality. Imagine you have a new neighbor you want to get to know. When you encounter each other, you smile and walk toward each other with interest and some caution. You don't know each other. You begin a simple conversation by inquiring about each other and occasionally hitting upon something you have in common. After a short while, you each go back to your day, respecting each other's time and glad for the introduction. Over time, you continue these neighborly conversations. You get to know each other well enough to invite each other into your homes, feeling comfortable and welcoming.

Developing mutual, respectful relationships with your gatekeepers is similar. Gentle approaching, careful listening, and honest understanding can, over time, have you comfortably spending time in your garden of self.

—

In this moment, think of a comfortable relationship in your life. What makes that relationship work so well?

142

Within your garden of self are multiple paths that access various aspects of you.

When you enter a garden, you often find paths within. In a vegetable garden, different paths might take you to lettuce, tomatoes, corn, and green beans. In a flower garden, there may be inviting walkways through the perennials leading to a bench by a fountain. There is texture and color and a feeling of beauty and growth.

So it is within you.

In your garden within are paths to various aspects of you. You are a composite of interests, talents, and knowledge. You have friendships, family relationships, and social involvement. You have dreams, needs, and goals. All of these are aspects of who you are, whether you are aware of them or not. There are more, too. Maybe you can think of a few more that are true for you.

Within your internal garden are paths to these various aspects of you and your life. Some of those paths may not be well established; it may be hard to see them. You may even have forgotten they were there as you traveled your more habitual and familiar paths.

Self-recovery is about improving your internal paths so you have solid access to the people, places, and things that are important to you. As you clear the paths—or even create new ones because the old ones are so overgrown—you can more easily get to the seeds you have planted for your self and then water, fertilize, and harvest what you are growing for you.

—

In this moment, what are some areas of your life you would like to improve the paths to?

143

Become your own internal trailblazer.

Trailblazers create a new path through the wild. They are pioneers and visionaries. They are realistic and take calculated risks. They see possibilities and respond to obstacles with resilience.

Self-recovery involves internal trailblazing.

Once you are in your garden of self, you may find clear trails that lead to important things you have planted there. You may notice less-maintained trails leading to other things you have planted. For example, a well-established trail might take you to your role as a parent or an employee. A less-maintained trail might take you to your exercise program or a book club. You get to those things sometimes, but not enough for the trail to be well-worn.

And then there are things you know you have planted in your garden, but you can't find a path to them. For example, perhaps you've always wanted to learn French but never have; you want to spend quiet time with your partner but never prioritize that; or you want eight hours of sleep but can't put yourself to bed.

Trailblazing is about improving and expanding your internal trail system so you can get to the things you have decided will enrich and strengthen you. Trailblazing fosters your self-attunement. Trailblazing involves awareness of your intended destination coupled with careful attention to the details of clearing your path each step of the way. With clarity, confidence, resilience, and commitment in your backpack, and openness and creativity in your hands, you can make some appealing new internal trails.

—

In this moment, is there something specific in your life you would like to clear a trail to?

144

Speak kindly to your self.

As you settle further into getting to know you, it is important to notice how you talk to your self. Progress on your internal trailblazing can be limited by what you tell your self. Critical, negative messages can be like a big tree that has fallen over the trail, making it a challenge to move forward.

At its core, codependency can be driven by beliefs we have about ourselves that keep us down: *That was stupid of me. I don't know what I'm doing. What I need doesn't matter. I'll never learn.* Often these messages have been with us a long time. They may have been said directly to us, or they may be what we concluded from our life experiences. Either way, our engrained beliefs about ourselves and the self-talk that comes from those beliefs can seriously limit our growth if those beliefs are judgmental and self-attacking.

Self-attunement involves speaking kindly to our self. We offer supportive self-regard through encouraging messages that convey patience and compassion: *I am smart and capable. I can do this. What I need is important, and I can give that to myself. I have learned a lot.*

You may not be aware of the things you are saying to yourself. They may be in the background or so habitual that you just don't notice them. Do your self a lasting favor and start paying attention to your self-talk. Does it promote feeling good and hopeful about you?

—

In this moment, notice the messages you are giving to you about you. Is your self-talk kind, patient, compassionate, and nonjudgmental?

145

Issues with control keep you entangled with others and not in tune with you.

It's time to talk about control and codependency. Control can be a slippery topic. Often, codependent people are trying to control what we can't (i.e., someone else) and we are not controlling what we can (i.e., our self). And too often we are not aware of our controlling behaviors as we roll on with our helping, fixing, and taking care of things.

As you try to control someone else, you become focused on them and lose contact with you. The more you try to control them, the more your focus narrows onto what you believe they should or should not be doing. As you slide down the behavioral continuum from okay to too far, relationship tangles ensue. Basically, no one likes to be controlled, so they are likely to resist. You don't like their resistance, especially if you believe you know best. The more you insist or force, the hotter the conversations become, and the possibilities for reasonable discussions and solutions go cold.

As this heated interaction develops, you are less and less in touch with you. Your ability to attune to your thoughts, feelings, and behaviors diminishes as the heat increases. Self-attunement becomes a distant possibility, even though it is what can save you from this tangle. You may have some good points; they may have some good points. But it is all pointless if you are not connected with you so you can think clearly, care for your emotions, and operate within respectful boundaries.

—

In this moment, can you think of a recent situation where you were trying to control someone else?

146

Sometimes what seems like helping is really controlling.

You may think you are just trying to help. You also may have some underlying reasons for helping that involve control, but you are not aware of your controllingness.

In its bolder forms, a controlling person appears bossy and in charge. They tell others exactly what they must do, or they simply take over. However, controlling behaviors can show up more subtly with codependency. Perhaps we are trying to hide our controllingness from others or from our self, or both.

Being controlling is not particularly attractive. We may believe that we are democratic, open-minded, and respectful of the freedom of all. But underneath those beliefs may lie some issues with control.

Maybe you are helping because:

- You want things to be done your way.
- You want things to be done the "right" way.
- You want things to be done now.
- You believe you are right.
- You believe you see what the other person can't see.
- You believe you know what is best for the other person.

As you look at these sneaky desires to manage and control, remember to be nonjudgmental. Control is a protective part of you that you are being invited to meet and greet more fully.

—

In this moment, how do you feel about the list of sneaky ways that control can be embedded in your offers to help?

147

Be aware of your motivations for what you say and do.

Since being controlling can be so hard to see, checking in with your motivations for what you say and do is very helpful. When you know what is behind your suggestions, requests, or actions, you are more self-attuned.

Motivations come in all shapes and sizes. We are motivated to help, caregive, fix, problem-solve, make things better, or get things done. We can also be motivated to have things our way. We may say or do things in order to control or change someone else. We may want them to feel a certain way or do something specific. We may try very hard to get the other person to like us or validate us. We might want them to tell us that they understand us or that they are not mad at us. There are so many layers of motivations woven within you that stem from your various life experiences and ways of relating.

Self-attunement involves increasing your awareness of what's behind those things you seek from others. What is motivating you? Once you are aware, you can decide how to proceed with your actions. You can choose to not help or engage with the other person, or you can assertively express what you want using a clear "I" statement. If you do assert your self, stay connected with your motivations, owning them and taking responsibility for them. When we don't have this level of self-awareness and ownership, we get tangled with others and lose our self.

—

In this moment, consider your motivations for reading this book. Are you reading it for you or with hopes of changing someone else?

148

You really can't change or fix someone else.

Being focused on someone else is a challenge to creating new paths within your garden of self. When your attention is on trying to get someone else to say or do something, you cannot clear paths for your own growth. In fact, your efforts to fix, manage, or control someone else can cause you all sorts of detours and setbacks.

As obvious as it sounds, as heavy as it feels, the reality is *you can't change or fix someone else.* Take a breath, and take this in. This may be unhappy news, or it may be great to hear. It may scare you, or it may free you. It may do both. Learning this at a deep level is part of self-recovery. We are all separate people with different biologies, backgrounds, life experiences, views, and styles. Acknowledging and respecting the individuality of each person is paramount for healthy relationships.

Be careful about entering a relationship with hopes that you can change the other person. A common codependent version of this is seeing the potential in someone and wanting to help them actualize that. It's a nice idea, but it is a strong invitation to let your attention be drawn to developing their life as your own life disappears. Also, the other person is probably not aware they are signing up for the improvement course you are designing specifically for them, so they may not be a willing student in your class.

It's best to design a self-improvement course for you.

—

In this moment, notice how you feel about the fact that you can't change someone else.

149

Put the Serenity Prayer into action.

When it comes to managing your controlling behaviors, you can't beat the Serenity Prayer:

God, grant me the
serenity to accept the things I cannot change, the
courage to change the things I can, and the
wisdom to know the difference.

This prayer is a useful tool for everyone, not just codependent people (and not just followers of a particular religion, as the beginning of the mantra can be changed to reflect your own beliefs). Unhappiness and frustrations often rise from trying to control what we have no control over. Somehow our misdirected efforts to manage and control other people escape us. We get lost in our desires and attempts to change someone else.

This prayer helps us know what to do with our controlling behaviors. In its few simple words, it has many important layers of guidance.

First, it invites discernment of what you can and cannot control. That's an important step already. Taking this step means you acknowledge that you can't control everything and are willing to examine what is in your control with a particular person in a particular situation.

Then, the prayer invites action on what you can control. It encourages you to courageously do what you have in your power to do.

Finally, the prayer invites you to let go of things that are not in your control—to metaphorically open your hands and release from your grip what you can't do anything about. Being able to let go may require multiple discernments of what you can and cannot control. It will certainly require willingness on your part to let go—willingness based on respect, faith, and your desire for the serenity the prayer offers.

—

In this moment, reread the Serenity Prayer, absorbing each line.

150

Use your wisdom to know what you can and cannot control.

Three important words in the Serenity Prayer are *serenity*, *courage*, and *wisdom*. Self-recovery is about all three, but in a different working order. Let's study wisdom first.

"Wisdom to know the difference" is how the word is used in the prayer. It refers to knowing the difference between what you can and cannot control. This is a fundamental lesson for the person in recovery from codependence—we are not in full control of everyone and all things. We know this on some level, but as we lose our self in someone else, we lose touch with this important basic of human relationships.

Here are a few suggestions to foster your wisdom, to help you discern what you can and cannot control:

- Pause or stop.
- Ground your self in the present moment.
- Connect with your diaphragmatic breath.
- Allow your calmness to help you think more clearly, completely, and realistically.
- Ask your self: *What in this situation with this person can I control?*
- Now ask your self: *What in this situation with this person is not in my control?*

To help you with your discerning questions, you may want to use the exercise from reading 94, where you draw a vertical line and place your self on one side of the line and the other person on the other. Put what is "mine" in your column; put what is "not mine" in their column. There—you did it. You have wisdom to know the difference.

—

In this moment, can you apply this discerning of what you can and cannot control to a current relationship of yours?

151

Use your courage to change the things you can.

The second line of the Serenity Prayer focuses on "courage to change the things I can." These seven words are so empowering. You can change you. Too often, our codependency has us fretting about what we can't change. But we *can* do something for our self. This is important to recognize and set as your base for your self-recovery.

To get started, tune into your needs, wants, feelings, and beliefs. Use the exercise from reading 94 to help you mentally separate you from the other person. Study what you have placed on your side of the line, what you have claimed as "mine." Or, using an imaginary balance scale with you on one end and the other person on the other end, notice what you have placed on your end of the scale as true for you. Now, with your focus on the "you" part of these images, consider what action or change you have the courage to make on your own behalf.

It is easy to write and read these words. It is inspiring to hear these things. But going ahead and taking action requires that you are willing, prepared, and committed to you. It means your sense of self is growing strong enough to lovingly assert and follow through with whatever you have discerned will help you: time with friends; time alone; a new job, class, or book; counseling; a support group; a retreat. These examples are all in your courageous control.

—

In this moment, can you think of a change you are ready to make that is in your control?

152

Enjoy the serenity of accepting what you cannot change.

Learning the difference between what you can and cannot change is big. Being able to accept what you cannot change is even bigger.

There are so many reasons we don't want to accept the things we can't change: hopes, dreams, expectations, invested time, protection from heartache, disbelief, rationalizations. We could explore these reasons and more, but let's look instead at a few ideas to help you accept what you cannot change—and, maybe, find your way to serenity as well.

- Once you have discerned what you can and cannot change, increase your awareness of how you feel when you are trying to control something you can't. Notice your internal cues when you are beating your head against a wall. For example: You can't stop thinking about what you cannot control. You keep trying new things with no success. You feel agitated and activated. Let your internal cues support what you know—that this is something beyond your control.
- Absorb the limitations of what you can do for or with someone else.
- Grieve the reality of these limitations. This reality will free you, though it may sadden or frustrate you at first.
- Cultivate a personal way or spiritual belief to which you can release what you cannot control.

Serenity is possible when you are able to accept the things you cannot change and let them go, knowing you cannot do more and turning those things over to something beyond you, however many times it takes.

—

In this moment, does serenity appeal to you?

153

Having trouble letting go of what you can't change?

Letting go is hard for many of us. We just don't want to give up. We care about the other person, want the best for them, and know there is a solution for them somewhere. We may even like the challenge of wrangling with something beyond our control. But at a point, that is not healthy for us or the other person.

Pursuing what is not in your control is an obstacle to self-attunement. As you pursue things you cannot change, your focus on you gets smaller and smaller. You leave you in the dust as you keep moving toward what you are determined to change. No need for blame; you're just bringing this into your awareness so you can change direction and move toward what you *can* change when you are ready.

Letting go of what you cannot control may take extra special steps. Here are some ideas for deeper releasing of what you cannot control:

- Write down on paper what you cannot control and then get rid of the paper in some way. Send it on its way, perhaps using one of the elements: wind, fire, air, or water.
- Imagine placing your ideas and wishes for the other person into their hands.
- Entrust what you cannot change to your spiritual beliefs.
- Say to your self, *Not mine.*
- Let go as you exhale.
- Use movement to walk off, shake off, or melt what is beyond your control.

—

In this moment, is there something you cannot change you would like to let go of using one of these ideas?

154

Letting go can be an invitation to lean further into your spirituality.

Self-attunement is about connecting with your self with sensitivity, responsiveness, and consistency. It means paying careful attention to your four areas of self—body, mind, emotions, and spirit—and making fine-tuned adjustments on a consistent basis that support your health and growth.

Your spirituality can be especially valuable to attune to as you work with letting go of things that are not in your control. The Serenity Prayer reminds us of this with its opening call: "God grant me . . ." You can change the word "God" to whoever or whatever may be a spiritual source for you, or simply begin the mantra with "Grant me . . ." This invitation to connect with your spirituality acknowledges how powerful controlling behaviors can be and the help you may need with them—help beyond your self.

Your spirituality is something to call upon. As you try to change what you can't, you may feel frustrated, sad, or alone. Your spirituality is there with you if you choose to connect with it. Your spirituality can offer listening, understanding, and comfort. It may give you another perspective or help you see what you have not been able to see.

Your spirituality is something to let go to. You can courageously release what you can't control to your spiritual sources. Your release involves trust and faith—not that things will work out as you wish, but that life will unfold as it will and that you can learn to live with what is, as you continue to grow in your self-recovery.

—

In this moment, how do you feel about leaning into your spirituality when you feel powerless?

Readings on

Your Relationship-with-Self

155

Your relationship with you is the heart of self-recovery.

You've heard about your relationship-with-self throughout these readings. It's time to zoom in fully on what that means. You've learned about the four elements of self-recovery—self-understanding, self-awareness, self-competence, and self-attunement. Remember, those four elements are visualized as circles that overlap to make a bigger circle. In the center of that self-recovery circle is your relationship-with-self. It is the heart of that image and the heart of your self-recovery work.

It is likely you often seek what you need from other people. This is quite normal. We are biologically wired for connection with others. Our relationships with others are important to our total health. However, as we've learned throughout these readings, many things are okay up to a point. This is true about seeking what we need from others—that, too, works up to a point, but not always. Codependency blossoms from seeking what we need from others. Untreated, codependency can lead us to lose our connection with self as we try to establish a connection with someone else that we hope will give us what we need.

Developing your relationship-with-self means establishing your connection with *you* so *you* can provide your self with what you need—love, security, kindness, respect, support, interest, confidence, and encouragement. Self-recovery is not a list of things to learn, do, and be done with. Self-recovery is a process of weaving the four elements of recovery together on a daily basis, ultimately creating a relationship with you that becomes the reliable, supportive foundation for your life.

—

In this moment, absorb the image of the four elements of self-recovery embracing your relationship-with-self in the center.

155

Self-Understanding
With compassion
Self-Awareness
Fostered by
calm presence
Relationship-with-Self
Self-Attunement
Established
with care
Self-Competence
With increasing
confidence

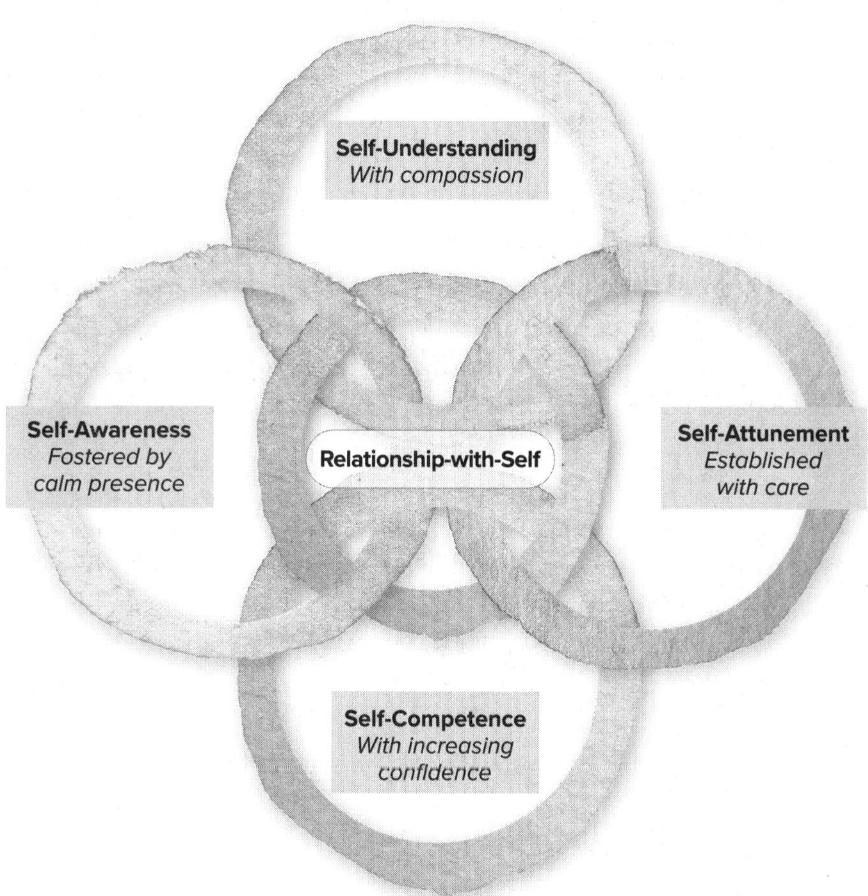

156

Yes, having a relationship-with-self is a real thing.

Someone asked, "Is having a relationship with your self a thing?" They were being humorous and curious. We sometimes speak of our relationship with our self casually, but rarely do we consider it to be as real as a relationship we have with someone else. To pull your self-recovery work together, it's time to make your relationship-with-self a real thing. It's time to develop it in the same ways you develop relationships with other people who are important to you.

Healthy relationships are based on a number of things: care for and interest in each other, patience, understanding, forgiveness, resilience, good communication, follow-through, staying in touch, trust, respect, and more. Here are some questions for you to consider as you develop your relationship with you:

- Do you truly care about you? Are you interested in what you have to say and want to do? Do you bring patience and understanding to your efforts to improve your life? Do you forgive your self when you don't like what you did? Do you keep moving forward?
- Do you have trust and respect for your self? Do you listen to your thoughts, emotions, and body? Do you respond to what you hear from you? If you are tired, do you rest? If you are sad, do you allow those feelings in safe ways? Do you stay in regular touch with you?

—

In this moment, take a few extra minutes with these self-reflection questions.

157

You are fostering your relationship-with-self.

Foster is such a lovely word. It sounds gentle and kind. It feels supportive and encouraging. It is about growth. We foster children, animals, and organizations. Why not foster our self, too?

Fostering your relationship-with-self invites even more intentional awareness and care than usual. Yes, as you have spent time with these readings, you have increased your self-awareness. You have learned more about you and have new skills you are practicing. Great work! And now, you are being invited to deepen your self-attunement.

Imagine you are fostering a dog. You prepare for the dog, bring it home, and change your routines to accommodate the dog's needs. You don't go off and forget the dog is there. You remember to feed and walk the dog and give it a comfy place to sleep. You speak kindly to the dog and help it learn how the two of you can live together in joy and peace. This is fostering.

Take any sentence from the previous paragraph and consider how you might offer your self the same level of fostering. Promoting the development of your relationship with you means you remember you, prepare for your needs, and provide for you on an ongoing basis. You speak kindly to yourself and welcome joy and peace within.

It will take time to build your relationship with you. All relationships are built over time. But it is so worth it. Your relationship-with-self will become a reliable source of safety, security, and care that will be yours to keep and continue to foster.

—

In this moment, what is one thing you can do to foster your relationship with you?

158

Meeting your true self is worthy work.

Deepening our relationship-with-self involves meeting and accepting our true self. Because of our strong external focus, many of us do not know our true self. For a variety of personal reasons, we learned to pay attention to and accommodate the needs of others. We attuned to the emotions of the people around us in order to protect our self from harm or abandonment, and as we did this, we ignored our own feelings. We absorbed how other people see us, what they believe we are capable of, and what they think we should do with our relationships and lives. No blame; just describing.

As you focused on the needs, emotions, and beliefs of other people, you did not get to know your true self. How could you? There was no time, space, or safety for that, no interest in or encouragement for you to be you.

But now you are creating that space and encouragement for your true self. Now you can listen to what you need and learn how to give that to you. You can attune to your emotions and offer your self emotional care. You can stop and think, *What would I like to do about that?* You can attune to your personal interests, preferences, and wishes for you. You can discard old, inaccurate messages you received about you and replace them with accurate and true statements as you get to know you.

For all things, you can ask your self, *What is true for me?*

—

In this moment, consider a decision you currently need to make and ask your self, What is true for me?

159

Imagine having a secure attachment with your self.

Self-recovery is about creating a secure attachment with your self. It is understandable if you deeply desire a secure relationship with someone else. That is human nature, and perhaps one day such a relationship will be yours. The path to that healthy, secure relationship with someone else is to first develop a secure relationship-with-self.

How do you do that, you ask? By offering your self the same qualities that a loving caregiver uses to create a secure attachment with their child—they are attuned, sensitive, responsive, consistent, warm, caring, trustworthy, confident, comfortable, and a safe haven. These qualities are helpful in that they point the way to you developing a secure relationship with your self.

First you have to be willing to make this commitment to you. You have to decide you want to be able to count on you, to know you will become a safe haven for your self in good and trying times. Then, as you learn to connect with you, you offer your self these same qualities that foster a secure attachment.

Having a secure attachment with your self is far from lame—it's an incredible strength. It gives you a readily available person to listen to you, comfort you, keep you safe, and guide you. A secure attachment with your self is a relationship you can come to trust and lean into for whatever it is you need at that time.

—

In this moment, can you imagine having a secure attachment with your self? How ready are you to work on being reliably there for you?

160

What are some qualities you want in your relationship with you?

When we are establishing a relationship, most of us have qualities we are looking for in the other person. Those qualities may include kindness, ease, mutuality, and loyalty. Think for a few moments about qualities you appreciate in an important relationship in your life. This could be with a parent, your children, another family member, or a friend. What qualities of that relationship allow you to feel safe and free to be your authentic self when you are with that person?

Think for another few moments about the qualities that can foster a secure attachment with your self: sensitive, responsive, warm, caring, trustworthy, and reliable, to name just a few. Which of these adjectives appeal to you in a relationship?

The question now is: Which of these qualities would you like to offer to your relationship-with-self? We know these qualities are desirable, yet we often do not bring them into the ways we talk to and treat our self. We get impatient with our self. We are critical of our choices. We don't even stop to completely listen to our self. Would you do any of these things to someone else you were in a relationship with? If you did, how would that go? What would happen to the relationship?

Coming back to your relationship-with-self, imagine speaking kindly to you. Imagine really caring about your welfare. Imagine relating to your self with interest and humor, confidence and trust. How would that go? What would happen to that relationship?

—

In this moment, identify several qualities you want to have in your relationship with you.

161

Consistently show up for you so you can count on you.

Consistency is everything. It's what makes things happen. It's what takes us to our goals. Have you ever had an exercise plan you were not consistent with? How about efforts to stop smoking or drinking? New Year's resolutions are good examples for many of us. We have the best of intentions, and then slowly but surely, we become inconsistent in whatever we were going to do differently, and then we completely stop.

As you develop your relationship-with-self, remember this: An important part of a secure attachment with you is connecting with you and being there for you on a *consistent* basis.

Consistently checking in with self is a challenge for most. As we first engage in self-recovery, we love the idea of stopping and noticing what we are feeling and thinking. It is new, exciting territory, and we feel the benefits of doing this. It is grounding. But then life calls, and off we go, leaving our self behind.

Your greater goal in self-recovery is to be in connection with your self in ongoing ways, not just occasionally or when you are upset. If you only seek out a friend when you need something from them, the relationship can sour. In contrast, consistent and ongoing connection supports secure relationship growth. And consistency teaches us we can count on something. Through consistent connection with you, you can become your own reliable source of love, comfort, and security. You can count on that!

—

In this moment, can you think of a way to remember to consistently check in with you over the course of a day?

162

Anchor in you.

Anchoring in self further establishes your relationship-with-self. Anchoring in self means making a commitment to stay connected with your body, mind, emotions, and spirit—a commitment to be attentive, supportive, and responsive to you as you live with and love others. The following meditation illustrates this connection and commitment.

> *An anchor holds a boat in place. The boat may rock and move around a bit, depending on the length of the rope to which it is attached. Nevertheless, the boat stays within the range of its anchoring, sometimes being pulled to the far edges of that range but not beyond. If we are on that boat, we trust that the anchor will keep us safe and where we want to be.*
>
> *Similarly, anchoring in self is not rigid. As with the boat's anchor, there is some range in which you are anchored to you. This range allows you to hear the other person, consider what they are saying, and remember the relationship you have and want to have with them. But listening does not mean pulling up your anchor and drifting away with the other person, leaving your relationship-with-self behind. Anchoring in self means knowing that you can stay within your internal safe haven and enjoy its secure benefits as you meet life's challenges and opportunities.*

—

In this moment, consider to what extent you are committed to you and your growth. Are you aware of any anchor within that helps to hold you in connection with you?

163

Develop your safe haven within.

With a secure attachment, your relationship with someone else provides a secure base from which you can explore and master the world, a safe haven that buffers against stress.

A safe haven—what a lovely image. It is wonderful when we have a safe haven in our relationships with others. And it is even more wonderful when we have it in our relationship with our self, because it can be there for us anytime.

Self-recovery is about developing a safe haven within you—a place to go to for compassion, calm presence, confidence, and care. With commitment and self-anchoring, you can develop your safe haven within.

Your safe haven can keep you safe from harm. It is a place where you can be curious and interested in you. You can cheer you on and make decisions that protect your mind and body.

Your safe haven can be a refuge. You can go there anytime you need or want to take a break and reconnect with you.

Your safe haven can be a storm shelter or a walk in the park. It can be both and more.

Visualizing your safe haven can be extra inviting and comforting. For example, your safe haven may be by the sea with gently rolling waves lapping onto the shore and a soft breeze on your face. Each of us experiences safety, security, and comfort differently. What is your image of a safe haven? What does that look like? Why is it a safe haven for you?

—

In this moment, if you wish, spend a few more minutes visualizing your safe haven within.

164

Give your self the things you wish for from others.

Codependency is about leaning too heavily on others for your purpose, identity, security, emotional regulation, confidence, or sense of self. You look outside your self too much for what you need and want. This creates a dependency on others that leaves you vulnerable, frustrated, lost, and sometimes empty-handed.

Self-recovery is all about learning to give your self what you are seeking from others. It's about becoming a reliable source of the things you need for a good life. It's about noticing what you are trying to get from someone else, and then redirecting you to you. For example:

- **Purpose:** If you are asking someone what they think would be a meaningful thing for you to do with your time and life, ask your self the same question. See what comes up that you are genuinely interested in and resonates for you. It may take some time.
- **Identity:** If you identify as someone's parent, partner, employee, and so on, that is fine, but in addition, who are you as a person?
- **Security:** If you are seeking reassurance from someone else, can you also reassure your self? Can you give your self the same interest and empathy you want so much from the other person?
- **Emotional regulation:** When your emotions are dependent on the emotions of someone else, that's a fragile situation for you. Learning how to care for your emotions separate from those of the other person gives you your own secure foundation.

—

In this moment, can you name something you are wishing for from someone else that you can give to your self?

165

You are becoming your own parent.

Your relationship-with-self is ultimately about becoming your own parent, teacher, therapist, and friend. To develop these internal relationships, first allow your self to experience, express, and process your feelings about what you did and did not receive from your parents or caregivers as you grew up. This is not about blame or staying stuck in unhappiness. It is about grieving and healing so you can move into authentic acceptance of your life experiences. Then, you can establish your relationship with your true self and create within you the type of secure relationship you seek from others.

You can become your own parent. You probably know what you liked and did not like about the parenting you received. The things you liked are the things you may want to use to parent your self. Maybe your parents showed interest in you, were patient, or forgave your mistakes. Maybe they listened well or encouraged you.

As for the things you did not like about the parenting you received, consider how you want to parent your self differently. Maybe your parents yelled, and you want to speak calmly. Maybe they were never around, and you want to make sure to be present for you. Maybe they said or did unkind things, and you want to be compassionate.

Sometimes as we parent ourselves, we speak to ourselves as our parents did. We hear their voices in our heads, both in tone and in message. Self-recovery involves intentionally becoming the parent you want to be for you. It's a great new opportunity to parent your self with new tones and messages that are helpful to you.

—

In this moment, what would you like your internal parent to be like?

166

You are becoming your own teacher.

Can you think of a teacher who made a difference in your life? It could be a teacher from school, church, or camp. It could be someone who taught you history, piano, woodworking, or soccer. Maybe you took formal lessons. Maybe you just hung out with them and learned a lot along the way.

With that person in mind, what made them a good teacher for you? Did they explain things well? Were they patient? Did they give you space to try out new things without judgment? Did they take time to understand you and the problems you were running into as you learned? Did they have confidence in you?

You are, in fact, becoming your own teacher. By spending time with this book of readings, you are teaching your self new things. Yes, the readings are teachers, but once you have finished a reading, it is up to the teacher in you to continue with the lesson.

And what does that look like? How do you teach yourself? Well, that is an individual process. Each of us learns in different ways. Take time to consider the type of teacher you work best with and the strategies that help you to learn. Remember the teacher who made a difference in your life and the qualities they brought to teaching you. Name strategies you successfully use to study and retain new material. Let the teacher within you know these things so you can become the best teacher possible for you!

—

In this moment, what would you like your internal teacher to be like?

167

You are becoming your own counselor.

Most of us have had a counselor at some point in our life. Counselors offer their services in a variety of settings: mental health clinics, schools, churches, camps, and social organizations, to name some of them. In each setting, the responsibilities and the emphasis of counseling work may vary, but there are core services most counselors provide:

- Counselors listen without judgment.
- Counselors are empathetic. They let you know they understand how you feel.
- Counselors are curious about you and want to get to know you.
- Counselors can see things you can't see because they are outside your story.
- Counselors know new facts and skills they can teach you.
- Counselors share their observations and thoughts without forcing them on you.
- Counselors help you understand your self in new ways as you are ready.

Counselors are there for you when you need them. Problems arise, moods get low, anxiety takes over, or relationships go sour. Counselors can help you through challenging times, but seeing a counselor is not a permanent relationship, for the most part. At some point, you resolve the problem, feel better, and grow on.

Then, it is time to use all that you learned from your counselor to become your own counselor. Instead of being dependent on them for support and guidance, you can offer your self those beautiful counseling services listed above. And guess what? You can schedule an appointment with your internal counselor anytime. They are on-call 24/7 just for you.

—

In this moment, as you study to become your own counselor, reflect on the list of counseling services above.

168

You are becoming your own best friend.

It may feel like it's becoming pretty crowded within you, after meeting all these internal characters: parent, teacher, counselor—and now, best friend. But really, all these internal characters are parts of you ready to serve and guide you as you do your self-recovery work. Remember, codependency is about being too focused on others; self-recovery is about having a solid connection with your self as you are in relationships with others. As you connect with you, these internal characters are there to help you out, and at least one of them is becoming your best friend.

We are all familiar with the term *best friend*. Many of us have been fortunate to have a few over our lifetime. Best friends are truly there for us when we need them. Whether they listen to us, cook for us, put us to bed, get help for us, or always remember our birthday, they are fellow human beings who we can count on. We know they will hold us, support us, and laugh with us. They will tell us the truth and cheer us on when we need to do something difficult. They want the best for us always.

You have probably been someone else's best friend and offered them these very same kindnesses. You would never have done differently for them. And so, why not offer all of these things to your self as well? You know how to be someone's best friend. How about becoming your own best friend, too? You've got this!

—

In this moment, write your self the same "thinking of you" note or text you would send to your best friend.

169

Your relationship-with-self enables you to have healthier relationships with others.

You have heard this said throughout these readings: your relationship-with-self improves your relationships with others. Sounds good. But you might be wondering how this works, when you feel selfish for focusing on you or guilty for setting a boundary with someone. All of this seems like it would upset the relationship apple cart.

Well, it does sometimes and to some extent—there's no denying it. Change is difficult for most people, and the closer it is to home, the more disturbing it may be. You are disrupting old patterns that may have served you well at one point in time but no longer help you and those in your life to grow. Those patterns may have protected you or created some needed stability. Now you need something different.

As you develop your relationship-with-self, you become a more complete person. You are aware of your thoughts, body, emotions, and spirit. You know your self more genuinely. You have grown into an adult who remains calm and clearheaded when in conflict, makes decisions not based on emotions or relationship pressures, acts in ways consistent with what you believe, and is clear about who you are without being pushy or wishy-washy.

With these strong features developed and in place, you can offer clarity, comfort, and engagement in your relationships without clinging, dominating, or disappearing. You can be present for the other person as you remain present for you. This makes for a fair, equal, and reliable relationship.

—

In this moment, what strengths can you now bring to your important relationships that make them healthier?

170

Your adult self can interact with others and represent you well.

Self-recovery is about becoming your own person. It's about individuating. It is about your circle-of-self being able to comfortably separate from the circle-of-self of someone else as you need and want to. It's about growing from enmeshment into your own being, a being that can be on its own *and* in relationship. Your adult self honors differences between you and others and treats your relationships with respect and mutuality.

As you become a more defined and stronger individual, you can:

- Have your own thoughts and opinions
- Express your thoughts and opinions
- Trust your own judgment
- Take responsibility for your life experiences
- Experience your self as a peer to others, not as below or above them

With these new abilities, you connect with what is true for you and share that with others. You state your ideas and needs without begging or demanding. You accept choices you have made and learn from them. You run things by others, but ultimately you get the last word on you. You do not feel like the underdog and lose your footing. You do not offend others by taking the upper hand. You speak and act for you. All of this represents you well and increases your chances of having healthy adult-to-adult relationships in your life.

Whether becoming an adult in these ways is a weight or a pleasure, or both, fostering the adult in you is the way to grow.

—

In this moment, reread the list of what the adult in you is able to do (on a good day).

171

You can resign from trying to make things happen.

Imagine letting go of something. Imagine the internal space or hours in a day you may gain. As you grow in self-recovery, your changes will lead to letting go of old patterns and habits such as trying to make things happen.

Trying to make things happen is a common behavior associated with codependency. We want good things for our self and others. So, we step in and take charge—scheduling appointments, making calls, working on the calendar, researching on the internet, spending money. We get so involved in what we want to happen that we lose track of the big picture.

Step back and consider the big picture. Do others want what you want? Have they said they would help to make it happen? Why do you want it so much? Will it benefit you as well as others? How much is it worth to you in time, money, and energy?

When we are trying to make something happen and it doesn't happen, it's likely not in our control. The moment you realize this is the moment to resign from trying to make it happen. You don't have to do more than your share. Do your part and let go of everyone else's. Yes, there will be consequences from what they do or don't do, but the consequences of not letting go are that you stay in your same old patterns and will likely become unhappy and resentful.

Consider resigning from trying to make things happen. No need to announce it to anyone but you.

—

In this moment, reflect on how you are when you are trying to make something happen.

172

You can let go of trying to keep everyone happy.

We can use codependency for our emotional regulation. What does that mean? Simply put, it means your emotions depend on someone else's emotions. If they are fine, you are fine. If they are upset, you are upset.

Emotional enmeshment may show up in several ways. We absorb the emotions of others. Or we need others to be okay because we feel responsible for their feelings. Or we need to protect our self from the other person's emotional states, so we pay attention to their moods, not ours.

As you develop your relationship-with-self, you become more aware of your emotions and the care they need from you. Your balance of self and others improves, and you feel the difference as you emotionally stuff less and attend to more.

With this growth, you can let go of trying to keep everyone happy. First, it is not possible to keep *everyone* happy. Second, you simply don't have the ability to make someone else happy. You cannot control the moods, thoughts, or behaviors of others. You have learned this. It's not bad news. It's just a fact. And so is the fact that you *can* focus your time, energy, and heart on making *you* happy. Likely that will make everyone else happy, too. Seriously—other people know when we are trying to improve their mood, and they really don't like it. They need us to back off and leave it to them. So, do that. And go take care of your own mood, whatever that may be.

—

In this moment, are you able to pay attention to your emotions and take care of them?

173

You can do less for others and give yourself more.

Many of us fill our days with activity. Some of our busy-ness is necessary work to live a good life: groceries purchased, meals cooked, clothes washed, money earned, and sleep gotten. Those activities alone are more than enough to fill a day. But often we have many more things going on, including things we do for others.

There is nothing wrong with doing things for others, but we can go too far with this. For example, we do things for others that they could do themselves. We do things for others that they have not asked us to do. We do things for others even though they told us not to.

When you pause and self-connect, you can notice if you are about to do any of these things and make a choice about what you want to do. Consider the other person, and equally important, consider you. What do you want your day to be like? What do you need?

Your self-reflections may well suggest that you do less for others and give your self more. That's self-recovery in action. That's when you are truly attuning to your relationship-with-self and responding to your needs and wants. As you balance self and others, you will find more time and space. Your invitation here is to not fill those spaces with things you can do for others but rather offer those precious minutes to you, even if there are only five or ten of them.

—

In this moment, watch for an opportunity today to fairly choose to give time to you.

174

Soak in all the good.

At this point, you are likely experiencing some of the benefits of self-recovery:

- Being more connected with your thoughts, body, emotions, and spirit
- Listening carefully to your needs and wants
- Feeling less shame and guilt
- Knowing how to express your self
- Setting more effective boundaries
- Believing in your value and the importance of taking care of you
- Discerning what you can and cannot control
- Accepting what you cannot control
- Acting on what you can control
- Understanding that balancing self and others is an ongoing process that is worthy of your effort, courage, and compassion

Solid self-recovery involves not only recognizing these changes in you but also letting the good from them soak into you. Notice how you feel when you are able to set a boundary or when you take a couple of hours just for you. Notice how you are when you let go of a situation you have no control over. Allow your self-compassion and kindness to seep in.

When something good comes our way, we too often rush on to the next thing or brush it off, minimizing the compliment or nice experience. Letting positivity seep in neurobiologically rewires you. Soaking up the good reinforces what is good in your life. You become more inclined to notice the good and make choices that promote more goodness for you and your relationship-with-self.

—

In this moment, make a list of the positive changes you are noticing in you. Then, spend at least one minute letting your good soak in.

175

Appreciate you.

You have been cultivating compassion, kindness, and openness for your self. Now, let's add appreciation to your relationship with you. *Appreciation* means you value what you are doing for you and for others. It means that, at a deep level, you recognize all you do to make your life better, and you thank your self for doing so.

We let other people know we appreciate them all the time. We point out something they did that made a difference in our life, and we thank them. We write them a note, send them a card, or maybe give them a small gift. We take them out for a meal or treat them to something they enjoy. We appreciate what they did, and we care very much to let them know this.

You are invited to do the same for your self. You are invited to appreciate the large and small things you are working on. You are invited to appreciate your efforts, your courage, and your compassion. Pause and notice all the things you are doing to make a difference in your own life. Find a way to recognize and thank your self for hanging in there when things are tough, for being there for you, and for becoming your own safe haven. Think of how to express your appreciation and gratitude to you, and then do it. Take your self out for a treat. Write your self a note. Buy your self some flowers or whatever delights you.

—

In this moment, spend some extra time with the last paragraph in this reading and see if you can think of an appreciation plan for you from you.

176

Your relationship with you is always evolving.

Relationships evolve over time. People get to know each other as they share personal stories, hopes, and dreams. Intimacy develops even as vulnerability is also present. Trust is earned, respected, and treasured. In a secure relationship, people learn they can count on each other.

Relationship challenges and setbacks are not uncommon along the way. We'd like to think we could reach a sweet spot in a relationship and it will stay that way. But this does not happen. Instead, as we say, life happens, and we make necessary personal and relationship adjustments. Ideally, the relationship is strengthened by weathering the disruptions together in fair and mutual ways.

This is also how your relationship-with-self evolves. You are just getting to know, accept, and appreciate you. You are becoming comfortable with the newness of checking in with you and knowing how to give your self attention, care, and respect. You are getting used to the idea of being there for you and are taking steps in that direction.

Your relationship with you will also be disrupted by life. You will have to give your full attention to someone else for some period of time. You will have to adjust your plans to accommodate others. But because you are building your relationship with you, all will not be lost. You will not be back at square one. You will settle down and reconnect with you, and the things you are learning will come back to you. You will once again listen to you with compassion and commit further to your evolving and ever-available relationship with you.

—

In this moment, how's your relationship with you going?

Readings on

Practices to Support Self-Recovery

177

Self-recovery can become your way of being.

Through these readings you have learned about the four elements of self-recovery: self-understanding, self-awareness, self-competence, and self-attunement. Each element is full of skills and insights to help you focus on you in new and effective ways. Perhaps you use some of the tools you have read about, or your self-reflections help you know and understand you better. You may feel more centered and less entangled with others. You may have more confidence and a clearer sense of self. This is what self-recovery offers.

To help you sustain your gains and keep growing, your next step is to make self-recovery your way of being. This means you connect with your self on an ongoing basis. You naturally stop and consider you. It becomes second nature to pause, connect with you, notice, reflect, and respond. You manage your guilt and assert your self as needed throughout your day. You intentionally say supportive things to your self. You live comfortably in your garden of self. You appreciate your relationship-with-self and celebrate the strength and security that relationship gives you. You value your growth and are committed to it.

Making self-recovery your way of being means you no longer operate from the programmed internal codes of codependency. You are aware and connected with you and others in real time. There is nothing habitual or automatic. You are paying attention and making choices from your centered, wise self. You are comfortable in your own skin and in your relationships because you know you can check in with you and count on you from one moment to the next.

—

Practice checking in with you in this moment.

178

Cultivate practices to support your growth.

As you grow forward, your commitment to you will be greatly helped by practices that help you stay actively in touch with what you are working on for you. Often, we hear good ideas but do not revisit or use them. Developing conscious ways to apply the ideas in these readings is essential to your ongoing growth.

Practices will help you kindly regard you and act on your own behalf rather than lose your self in others. Practices will help you successfully shift from overfunctioning for others to better balancing what you do for you and others.

Practice means a couple of things.

Practice means go ahead and *try* some of the ideas in these readings so you can learn how to do them and see if they work for you. Give your self an intentional assignment. Rehearse asserting your "I" statements or setting a boundary. Use the exercise in reading 94 to separate what is yours from what belongs to someone else, or study the behavioral continuum described in reading 14 to see if you are going too far with your behaviors associated with codependency. Think of a practical way to remind your self to check in with you at least once per day.

Practice also means making these ideas *the way you live your life*. Through regular practices, self-recovery can become an increasingly satisfying way of being for you. You will naturally incorporate your self-recovery work into the way you greet your day, your relationships, and the world. This is the practice of self-recovery.

—

Practice at least one idea that you have read about and may want to make a regular part of your life.

179

With patience and kindness, you can learn to be in connection with you much of the time.

Patience and kindness go a long way in helping you make reliable and supportive connections with you. This may sound obvious. It may even sound too sweet. But it is true.

We are often impatient with our self. We think we should have learned all these things a long time ago. Or we think we should be able to immediately use a new skill with resounding success when in fact we are trying to change long-standing patterns and ways of being. One quick read will not be enough to alter those patterns. Time, patience, and practice will.

We are often judgmental with our self. We believe we are hopeless. We tell our self we will never learn or don't have what it takes to be strong and well. We may try new things, and then we criticize what we did. We give our self messages like *I could have done better* or *I don't think I did a good job*. Judgment stops us. Judgment shames us and keeps us hiding out, even—and especially—from our self.

Patience and kindness open doors and invite us in. Patience and kindness are interested and empathetic. They are supportive and comforting. They give you space to listen to you, encourage you as you make changes, and create an internal environment of love and acceptance that is yours no matter what is happening outside of you. This is the heart of self-recovery.

—

Practice patience and kindness with you.

180

As you cycle through the elements of self-recovery, your work will deepen every time.

The four elements of self-recovery—self-understanding, self-awareness, self-competence, and self-attunement—are not a list to be completed and checked off. As you have learned, they are overlapping circles in a circle. They are in a circle because you move from one element to another as needed throughout your day and with your growth. They overlap because each element supports the other elements.

For example, you may use self-awareness to help you recognize which new skills you need in self-competence. You may use what you have learned in self-understanding to help you deepen your relationship with you through self-attunement. Self-attunement work is fostered by self-awareness.

These interacting elements reflect the dynamic way this process of self-recovery works. Instead of it being a one-and-done process, you will find that each day, each moment, invites you to visit one or more of the elements for resources that will help you connect with and consider you.

Each time you do this, you will deepen your self-recovery work. Each time you remember to become self-aware or to self-attune, you will grow. Each time you use a new skill or compassionately understand why you did something, you will grow. You will be reinforcing what you have learned, practicing it more, and neurobiologically changing your wiring in the direction of new thoughts, emotions, and behaviors that support the growth you seek.

—

Practice an idea from each of the four elements over the course of today.

181

You can enjoy your garden of self.

Your garden of self is a metaphor for all that is within you. It represents what you, the gardener, are planting, nurturing, and harvesting for your growth. As you grow in your self-recovery, your visits to your garden of self can be more frequent and longer. You have gotten to know many of your gatekeepers and have workable, even supportive, relationships with them that allow you to comfortably enter and spend time in your internal garden anytime you wish. And you know how to meet and greet a new gatekeeper who may not have shown up before.

Now is the time to experience your garden of self more fully. Let your senses take in what is good and growing there. What do you see in your garden? Is there color? Is there variety? Do you notice any particular sounds? Are there things to smell? Is there something for you to snack on? Can you feel the air around you or objects in your hands you may have picked up along the paths?

Equally important, how do you, the gardener, feel in your garden? Do you experience more comfort and ease? Are you glad to be there? Do you feel restless to leave? Are your gatekeepers telling you that you've been there long enough?

No matter what your senses and experiences are in your garden of self, you have made great progress in cultivating it and spending time there. Keep it in mind. It is always there waiting for you to visit for however long you wish.

—

Practice spending time in your garden of self.

182

Intentionality carries the weight of growing forward.

The first three ingredients of change are awareness, willingness, and intentionality. These ingredients are with you and in action already. Your awareness of your strong focus on the needs, moods, and behaviors of other people brought you to this book. Your willingness to learn about this imbalance and to make changes in you has kept you reading. Intentionality now carries the weight of growing forward.

Intentionality means creating the time and energy for the practices needed to make self-recovery your new, natural way of being. This involves commitment to you and the process these readings have gently laid out. Reading by reading, piece by piece, you are learning new tips and tools, ideas, and imaginings for you. Your personal assignment now is to revisit them, practice them, and pause long enough to remember to use them in your daily life.

Intentionality means doing something on purpose. It means you make a plan, set a goal, create reminders of your work, and have a way to be accountable to your self. Imagine that. Sometimes we expect others to be accountable without asking the same of our self. If that has been the case for you, there's no need for judgment here—just new awareness.

We may wish we could be changed simply by reading these new ideas. Reading helps, but intentional practice is necessary for further growth. Without intentionality, we easily slip back into our usual ways of thinking, feeling, and acting. Those are well-worn paths. Practicing self-recovery on purpose is needed to strengthen the wiring of your internal focus, which builds that reliable relationship with you.

—

Practice doing something intentional today.
Pick it. Plan it. Do it. Notice how that feels.

183

Make sure you remember your goals for you.

Goals anchor us in what we are doing and where we are headed. Whether it is a goal for today or for this month, having a goal identifies a specific, intentional action.

We usually set goals when we want to make a change, like stop a habit or learn something new. If we are not careful, we set goals beyond what we can reasonably do. Yes, we are motivated and want fast results. But it is not helpful in the long run to make big and broad goals.

Solid goals are specific and realistic. *Specific* means you name the exact action or behavior you have in mind, along with clear amounts and frequencies. For example, you may decide to go to the gym for one hour per day, three times per week. To be more specific, you can name the days of the week and time of day you will go.

Realistic means this is a goal you can really pull off. It means you have enough time, energy, and other needed resources—like money, childcare, or transportation—to be successful. In the example above, the goal to go to the gym for one-hour sessions three times a week is realistic for many people; an unrealistic goal would be to go to the gym for three-hour sessions seven days a week. These are just examples. Each person has to figure out what they can realistically do.

Then we do it. We remember our goals and plan our days accordingly. And occasionally we revisit our goals to ensure we are realistically headed in our desired direction.

—

Practice setting a specific, realistic goal for you—something you really care about.

184

Create reminders for tuning into you.

For self-recovery to become your natural way of operating, tune in to you on a regular basis. This is your foundation for recovery. This means turning your focus inward a number of times and in various ways over the course of the day. Notice your self amid your daily activities. When you have a strong emotion, pause and connect with you. If you are confused, settle and listen to your varied thoughts and feelings compassionately and patiently.

Staying connected with you can be a challenge. We often run away from our self by focusing on our to-list for the day, not noticing how these demands are affecting us. We get stuck in negative thought patterns, letting them drag us down so we become unhappy or anxious about things that may not even be happening. We experience strong emotions and let them influence what we say and do, which we sometimes regret or feel guilty about.

Reminders to tune in to you can be quite helpful. You can program a reminder into your phone—rather than an "alarm," think of it as a bell of mindfulness—that brings you to the present moment, wherever you are and whatever you may be doing. You can post reminders in places you will notice them. You can associate tuning-in with routine activities such as brushing your teeth, getting into the car, or sitting down to eat. Even noticing your very breath can be a distinct reminder and invitation to pause and connect with you.

—

Practice creating a reminder to help you tune in to you regularly throughout the day.

185

Create self-assignments that keep you on your track.

We have all had homework. Whether it was assigned by school teachers, physical therapists, or piano instructors, we know what it is like to be given specific things we are supposed to do to make progress. We also know that we don't necessarily love having to do homework, and sometimes we are not so great about getting it done.

Whether we run toward it or not, homework serves important purposes. It asks us to spend time with the new material, practicing it and becoming more proficient in whatever it is that we are learning. We are fooling our self if we think we will show improvement at our next piano lesson if we have not practiced.

Self-recovery involves homework, too. With self-recovery, homework works best if you assign it to your self. You know what you need to reread or practice or learn more about. You may have to pause to figure out your self-assignments, but doing so personalizes them. Then, you will be more invested in getting your homework done. You know how it will help you.

Create self-assignments regularly that support the things you want for you. Here are a few ideas to get you started:

- Journal in whatever way you wish.
- Draw, color, or paint to express your self.
- Read a book that supports what you are working on.
- Spend time with friends.
- Get up and move.
- Check out something you have been curious about.

—

Practice giving your self a homework assignment.

186

Daily practices can really help you with the changes you want.

Doing something each day to support your self-recovery goes a long way toward the new, balanced lifestyle you want for you. Think of the things you already do each day: eat meals, brush your teeth, get some sleep, check your phone. These things have become automatic. They are woven into the fabric of your day. They each serve a purpose, which you no longer have to think about because they are such a part of you now.

Daily practices for self-recovery are invitations to pause, connect, notice, reflect, and respond. As you do them, you will develop your ongoing, organic connection with your self so eventually you won't have to stop and intentionally practice. And these practices don't have to be long. They can be as quick as brushing your teeth or checking your phone. But don't do them while you are doing these or other things. When you spend time with a self-recovery practice, stop and give your full attention and intention to your practice. Here are some ideas for daily practices to jump-start your own ideas:

- Read daily reflections that support your changes.
- Actively journal—whatever that means to you.
- Intentionally pause and connect with your mind, body, emotions, and spirit.
- Connect with people who understand the work you are doing for you.
- Connect with your strengths, your wise self.
- Notice what you need in the moment and respond to that, if possible.

—

Practice one thing daily for the next week to support your self-recovery. Pick something you can commit to, and build in a way to remember to do it.

187

Reading these readings is a practice in itself.

You have already developed a regular practice by reading these readings. Well done!

How did you do it? What within you knows this is important to you? What do you do to make sure you keep reading? These questions help you identify your strengths, which have gotten you this far in your self-recovery and which you can build on growing forward.

In order to establish a regular practice, we must be in touch with why we want to do it and how it will benefit us. And we must keep these reasons in mind and heart, since life will inevitably distract us from what is genuinely important to us.

We are also helped with our regular practice by creating some structure that reminds and supports our practice. For example, perhaps you will keep this book in a specific place where you know you will pick it up, or maybe you choose a time of day that is best for you to sit for a few minutes and absorb the messages here.

Now take a minute to reflect on what it is like for you to spend regular time with these readings. Step back and think of readings you have liked and want to remember. Consider how you were when you first got this book and how you are now. Any answers are fine, because they are *your* answers, *your* experiences—that's what these readings are all about. Sustaining a regular practice involves paying attention to what you are getting out of it. As you experience benefits from your practice—even small ones—let that good seep in, and read on.

—

Practice noticing what you are getting out of these readings.

188

Find times to stop and breathe mindfully.

You are breathing all the time. It is your very life connection. How about you use it as your self-connection as well? All you have to do is bring awareness to the cycles of your breath. This immediately connects you with you in the present moment. This is mindfulness.

Here is a bit of guidance to help you understand this practice and enrich your experience.

- Stop whatever you are doing for a few minutes. Put down anything in your hands and set aside anything that would interrupt you.
- Sit, lie down, stand, or walk.
- Bring your attention to your breath.
  - Breathe in through your nose and out through your mouth.
  - Follow your natural breath cycle. You are not trying to make it deeper. It will deepen on its own.
- Notice the sensations of air as it enters your body and as it leaves. Let this be your anchor to the present moment.
- If thoughts arise—and they will—notice them and then bring your focus back to your breath. You will do this more than once. This is a training program.
- Be nonjudgmental and patient with you and your experiences as you practice.
- Spend three to five minutes following your breath in this way.

Mindfulness brings mind, body, and breath together, helping you to be more centered and in direct connection with you.

—

Practice these suggestions for mindful breathing at least once a day.

189

Notice the messages you are giving your self.

How are you? Can you answer this question without judging or attacking you? Can you connect with you in genuinely curious, kind, and supportive ways?

Over the course of our day, we lose our self in all that we are doing. We may have a schedule to keep, meetings to prepare for, family to spend time with, and that exercise program we want to start. As we move from one activity to the next without a pause, our self-awareness gets smaller, and finally, we probably aren't in touch with our self at all.

When we stay so busy, we often do not hear the messages we are giving our self. It is likely, though, that somewhere within, you are fussing at your self for all you are doing, criticizing your efforts, or telling your self you just can't change. These messages do not support self-recovery. They keep you stuck in your usual ways and make you even more unhappy.

Make sure the messages you are giving you support self-regard. Notice your self-messaging when you are busy, or notice it when you take your intentional pauses to connect. If you are fussing, criticizing, or discouraging your self, see if you can modify that self-talk to convey appreciation and encouragement: *You did a good job on that. You are moving in the right direction.* And if you find that you are already saying supportive things to you—like *You said that well* or *I know you can do this*—you can then add, *Keep up the good work!*

—

Practice saying something supportive to you about you.

190

Notice your gatekeepers when they show up, and greet them.

Sometimes you can't miss the gatekeepers when they show up. You might be trying to pause and connect with you, and one of them says, "You don't have time to do this!" You might be about to say no to something, and a gatekeeper says, "They will never ask you again." You might in the midst of tuning in to your emotions, and another gatekeeper says, "What's the point of this?"

Sometimes our gatekeepers show up in our behaviors, many of which are habitual. We stay busy. We step in and take over. We want to fix or please. We do things for others they did not ask us to do.

As you continue to grow, keep noticing your gatekeepers as they show up. They are not there to stop you from growing. They are old protectors who are still on duty. You won't know what they are protecting you from until you greet them.

So, as you move forward with your next recovery action, notice when some old message or behavior shows up that wants to take you away from what you are trying to do. It's probably a gatekeeper at the entrance to your garden of self who comes out of its gatehouse and wants to know what you are up to.

Breathe, smile, and center your self. Clearly and patiently explain why you want to travel into your garden. This gatekeeper is part of your internal community. It lives and works within you every day. It's time to notice it, greet it, and start building a workable relationship.

—

Practice meeting and greeting one of your gatekeepers today.

191

Keep working on your relationships with your gatekeepers.

Just as with any relationship you value, you will spend time getting to know your garden-of-self gatekeepers and learning what makes your relationship with each of them work. You will be maintaining the relationships you have established, and new gatekeepers will show up. This is an ongoing process.

Maintaining relationships is important and takes more than we realize. If we are not careful, we can take a relationship for granted. We trust it will be there. We have made a commitment to it, and we are living in ways that are consistent with that commitment. But we can fail to intentionally spend time with that person, to give them our full attention, or to let them know we appreciate them. All of these actions deepen the relationship and reassure the person that our relationship with them is valuable to us.

As you continue to encounter your gatekeepers, stop and spend a bit of time with them. Give them your full attention. Ask how they are feeling about the ways you all have worked things out so you can go within. Ask how they are feeling about their new gatekeeper jobs you all have negotiated. Tell them how you, the gardener, are feeling about being able to spend time in your garden within and how that is benefiting you. Thank them for all they have done over the years to protect you and for the new, improved relationship you now share.

—

Practice a visit with one of your gatekeepers you have come to know and have a workable relationship with.

192

You will still be challenged by the draw of things outside of your self.

There is no magic solution here. There is no way to permanently balance your care of self and others so you do not have to work at it again. We all wish that were so, but life happens. You will still be drawn by people and things outside of you. The needs, requests, worries, and upsets of others will be a part of your daily life.

Usually these are people you know and care about, so it's normal to want to reach out and help them in some way. That's okay. It's your human nature in action. Self-recovery is not about ignoring their needs or cutting them out of your life.

Self-recovery *is* about not losing your self in whatever outside of you has drawn your attention. It is about keeping your connection with you even as you are in relationship with others. As you listen to them and feel for them, simultaneously listen to you and notice your own feelings. As you offer to help them, stay connected with what you need as well.

This reminder of daily external challenges is not meant to be discouraging, but rather realistic. It highlights the value of your self-recovery work in ongoing and ever-deepening ways. With commitment to you and regular practices, you can handle these challenges coming at you. You can keep your feet under you, your mind clear, and your heart open to all—including, and especially, you.

Self-recovery helps you be ready for life as it happens.

—

Practice noticing something that draws you away from you and how you handle you and that situation.

193

There will be natural opportunities to practice what you are learning.

Practices are often intentional. We set a goal, create an assignment, and take action. We try out a new skill or settle into a reflective daily practice. All of this is good. We learn new things and change old patterns.

But sometimes we are presented with a natural opportunity to use what we are learning. All of a sudden, a situation presents itself, and we can choose to do our same old thing or practice something new and different. Sometimes we are aware of this choice. Sometimes we just naturally speak and act in our new ways. Words come out of our mouth in centered, clear ways that surprise us. All our preparation has made us ready for this moment.

For example, perhaps you have been preparing to tell your partner about your plans to take a class next semester. You are worried about their reaction. Then, one morning over coffee, your partner suggests a trip when your class begins. Your natural opportunity has arisen to tell them your plans using what you have learned and rehearsed.

Or perhaps you feel angry about something your friend said to you. You did not tell them your feelings then. You decide to let them know how you feel, but you don't know when that will be. Then, you get a text from them suggesting you get together. You choose to use this natural opportunity to talk on the phone and tell them your feelings.

Every day offers natural opportunities for practicing what you are learning.

—

Practice noticing a natural opportunity to say or do something you have been preparing for.

194

Self-reflection is a great way to connect with you.

You have already been doing plenty of self-reflection through these readings. It's time to name self-reflection as a tool and talk about how it helps you deepen your practice of self-recovery.

Self-reflection means you stop and tune in to your thoughts and feelings about something. You reflect on it. For example, say you just went on a nice vacation. In general, you know you enjoyed it. When you stop and reflect on it, you may find more thoughts and feelings within. You may realize that it was the trip of a lifetime, and you are so grateful you did it! You may identify things you would do differently on your next trip. You may remember meaningful conversations during the trip that slipped your mind earlier. All of this enriches your experiences and the depth to which you are in touch with you.

Self-reflection is not self-judgment. It is not about being harsh with or hard on you. Self-reflection is about checking in with your self with curiosity and openness. It is about living your day and looking back on how things went. It is about considering how you feel about an interaction with someone. It is about speaking up in new ways and then tuning in to how you feel about what you said and how it went.

Self-reflection provides valuable information to help you grow forward. It encourages you to take in the good, to learn from your experiences, and to become even more connected to you.

—

Practice self-reflection by noticing how you feel about this reading.

195

Notice your self in the moment.

As self-recovery becomes a way of being, you will connect with your self more frequently and comfortably. You will naturally and spontaneously tune in to you in the midst of your activities over the course of a day. You will learn to *notice your self in the moment*, an additional ongoing self-recovery practice.

Notice your self in both quiet and active moments. In quiet moments, bring a caring curiosity to how you are feeling and what you are thinking. Notice the messages you are giving your self about you, making sure they are supportive and responsive to your needs.

In active moments, when something draws your energy and focus away from you—whether internal or external activity—check in with you in that moment. Your reactions to things that disconnect you from you are solid cues to pause, go within, and reconnect with you. For example, if you have a strong emotion, pause and be with it. If you feel compelled to do something, pause and consider your options.

Being able to pause depends on noticing what you are experiencing in the first place. Pausing then opens the door to even more self-awareness. It gives you space between what disturbed you and what you want to do about it. You can reconnect with your reasons, values, and goals. You can respond rather than react.

Noticing self in the moment can be a lovely way to live. You are your own companion in life, checking in with how you are, identifying what you need, and tending to those things moment by moment.

—

Practice noticing your self in this moment.

196

Intervene on your own behalf.

With the self-awareness you are developing, you can now use another self-recovery practice for ongoing growth: *Intervene on your own behalf.*

An intervention is a caring process designed to connect a person with the treatment they need. For example, in an intervention for addiction, concerned family and friends carry out a well-planned meeting with their loved one to explain their worries and request treatment for them. It's rare for an intervention to be done for a person with codependency . . . but sometimes we need one! And that's usually up to us. Learning to intervene on our own behalf can be life-changing. Here's how we do it.

Noticing self in the moment sets the stage for your self-intervention. The moment you notice a strong emotion, an old pattern of pursuing or retreating, or an irresistible preoccupation, this is the moment to intervene on your own behalf. Once you notice these types of cues, you have the opportunity in that moment to do something different than you usually do. You can stop, take a break, leave, say something different, or say less.

Intervening on your own behalf brings your self-recovery tools fully into play. It involves a rerouting of you in the moment from your usual to your new. It is about literally recovering your self in this precious moment when change and growth are possible. When you are *with* your self, not *beside* your self, you can intentionally stop your usual reactive behaviors and do something different that supports the changes you seek.

—

Practice intervening on your own behalf sometime today when you notice a moment when you could do the same old thing or something new.

197

Recognize your progress.

Noticing what you are accomplishing is very important. It is easy to lose your self in the challenges of the day, in the next problem to solve, in some disappointment. As you move from one thing to another, you lose touch not only with your self in general but with your progress specifically. It can feel like you have not learned a thing—but you have, no doubt!

One way to do this self-assessment is to look at your original goals when you started reading this book. With those goals in mind, what is better for you? Perfection is not what we are after. Progress, however small, is what deserves credit. So, what is better? Maybe you catch your self sooner when you are about to overextend your self, even if you still have trouble stopping. Maybe you know how to set a boundary but can't yet act on that. This is progress.

Another way to assess your progress is by completing self-statements such as the following:

- I used to ______, but now I . . .
- I am noticing that I now . . .
- What is working for me is . . .
- I feel good when I am able to . . .
- I surprise myself when I . . .

What self-statements come to mind as you reflect on all the growth and care you have cultivated for your self?

Recognizing your progress and really taking it in supports long-term change. It is a deeper form of self-awareness that invites you to give your self credit for what you have gained. And it helps you to see the foundation upon which you are building your relationship-with-self.

—

Practice recognizing your progress.

198

Absorb the good progress you are making.

Noticing your progress is self-awareness. Absorbing it and believing in you is self-attunement. Your secure relationship-with-self grows from these actions.

Let what works for you seep in. Don't just think, *Yeah, I was able to do that* or *That worked out well*, and then move on to the next thing. Stop for 30 seconds and really take in whatever you felt good about. Try not to critique your progress, telling your self you could have done better. Just let the good seep in.

The good is anything you feel encouraged or positive about as you look at your progress, no matter how small or whether anyone else sees it. If *you* recognize it, that's what matters.

If you notice you feel more grounded, let that awareness seep in. Take a mindful breath. Inhale fully. Then, let your exhalation travel throughout your body, flushing out tension and fear and grounding you in the present moment.

If you are able to think more clearly when you are upset, spend a bit of time recalling a specific experience of this. Color in that experience with all that you can remember—both actions and feelings. Remember the details of what you said, how you felt, and how you took care of you as you communicated with the other person. Notice what worked for you and how you did that.

Absorbing your progress is good for your body and your spirit. Your body reprograms itself toward the positive and your spirit carries you to hope and belief in you.

—

Practice absorbing a piece of progress you are making.

199

Continue to foster your relationship with you.

Everything about self-recovery is taking you to your relationship-with-self. Codependency is about having a strong focus outside of your self, accommodating others at your own expense. With codependency, you can be so focused on your relationship with someone else that you forget about your relationship with you.

You are changing that moment by moment, day by day. That's how recovery works.

Your ultimate goal is to naturally stay in connection with you and offer your self the support and action you need. You know you can count on you to come through for you. You know your healing path and have the skills needed to travel your new internal parkways. You experience a sense of groundedness, comfort, and security that is totally yours.

Reaching these goals involves continually fostering your relationship with you. This means you care about you, believe in your value, and want the best for you. It means you intentionally remember your relationship-with-self. Create reminders around you of this relationship you are fostering: post notes to you, set bells of mindfulness on your phone, or let some daily activity remind you to check in with you. Have active, ongoing self-connectivity with curiosity and willingness, trust and consistency, playfulness and fun.

How will you stay in touch with you? What will help you to remember and sustain this most important relationship—your relationship with your self?

—

Practice one thing that will help you stay in touch with you.

200

You. Here. Today.

The first reading in this book had this same title: *You. Here. Today.* That was a fitting title to begin with and is a fitting title to conclude with. You are finishing this book, but not your self-recovery journey. You will travel on, and you can use *You. Here. Today.* as your daily reminder to kindly connect with you.

You. This is your invitation to bring your focus to you in balance with the attention you pay to others. It reminds you of your value and the importance of listening to your body, thoughts, emotions, and spirit. Doing so helps you think clearly, make solid decisions, and respond to your body and soul.

Here. This is your invitation to be in the present moment. Yes, there are disturbances from yesterday. Yes, you have to plan ahead. But in the present moment, you can calm your self, clear your head, and offer balanced responses rather than impulsive reactions. Responding helps you interrupt your old patterns of overfunctioning for others and instead act on your own behalf as well.

Today. This is an invitation to have an accurate, compassionate understanding of who you are now. As you grow, you may feel upset about how long it took you to figure things out. Or you may feel impatient, wanting to grow further and faster than you have. Today is today. How are you today? Can you identify some changes you have made? Are there ways you feel different, maybe even better? Do you have a new confidence or peace within, even sometimes? Just notice who you are here and now, and honor your efforts and good work.

—

Practice You. Here. Today.

Resources

Ainsworth, M. D. S., Blebar, M. C., Waters, E., & Wall., S. N. (2015). *Patterns of attachment: A psychological study of the strange situation.* Psychology Press.

Al-Anon Family Groups. (1987). *One day at a time in Al-Anon.*

Altman, D. (2019). *Reflect: Awaken to the wisdom of the here and now.* PESI Publishing.

Baranowsky, A. B., & Gentry, J. E. (2014). *Trauma practice: tools for stabilization and recovery* (3rd ed.). Hogrefe Publishing.

Beattie, M. (1987). *Codependent no more: How to stop controlling others and start caring for yourself.* Hazelden.

Beattie, M. (1990). *The language of letting go: Daily meditations for codependents.* Harper & Row.

Beck, J. S. (2020). *Cognitive behavior therapy: Basics and beyond* (3rd ed.). The Guilford Press.

Black, C. (2020). *It will never happen to me: Growing up with addiction as youngsters, adolescents, adults* (3rd ed.). Central Recovery Press.

Bowen, M. (1978). *Family therapy in clinical practice.* Jason Aronson.

Bowlby, J. (1988). *A secure base: Clinical applications of attachment theory.* Routledge.

Brown, B. (2007). *I thought it was just me (but it isn't): Telling the truth about perfectionism, inadequacy, and power.* Gotham Books.

Brown, B. (2018). *Dare to lead: Brave work. Tough conversations. Whole hearts.* Vermilion.

Burns, D. (2020). *Feeling great: The revolutionary new treatment for depression and anxiety.* PESI Publishing.

Co-Dependents Anonymous International. (2011). *Patterns and characteristics of codependence.* https://coda.org/meeting-materials/patterns-and- characteristics-2011

Dana, D. (2018). *The polyvagal theory in therapy: Engaging the rhythm of regulation.* W. W. Norton & Company.

Dana, D. (2020). *Polyvagal exercises for safety and connection: 50 client-centered practices.* W. W. Norton & Company.

Fisher, G., & Harrison, T. (2018). *Substance abuse: Information for school counselors, social workers, therapists, and counselors* (6th ed.) Pearson.

Fisher, J. (2021). *Transforming the living legacy of trauma: A workbook for survivors and therapists.* PESI Publishing.

Fisher, J. (2022). *The living legacy of trauma flip chart: A psychoeducational in-session tool for clients and therapists.* PESI Publishing.

Gentry, J. E. (1999). *Trauma recovery scale (TRS).* https://ebchelp.blueprint.ai/en/articles/8264356-trauma-recovery-scale-trs

Gilbert, R. M. (2004). *The eight concepts of Bowen theory: A new way of thinking about the individual and the group.* Leading Systems Press.

Graham, L. (2018). *Resilience: Powerful practices for bouncing back from disappointment, difficulty, and even disaster.* New World Library.

Greenberg, M. (2016). *The stress-proof brain: Master your emotional response to stress using mindfulness and neuroplasticity.* New Harbinger Publications.

Hanson, R. (2009). *Buddha's brain: The practical science of happiness, love, and wisdom.* New Harbinger Publications.

Hanson, R. (2009, November 1). Taking in the good. *Greater Good Magazine.* https://greatergood.berkeley.edu/article/item/taking_in_the_good

Hanson, R. (2013). *Hardwiring happiness: The new brain science of contentment, calm, and confidence.* Harmony Books.

Johnston, N. L. (2012). *My life as a border collie: Freedom from codependency.* Central Recovery Press.

Johnston, N. L. (2020). *Disentangle: When you've lost your self in someone else* (2nd ed.). Central Recovery Press.

Johnston, N. L. (2024). *The clinician's codependency treatment workbook.* PESI Publishing.

Kabat-Zinn, J. (2005). *Wherever you go there you are: Mindfulness meditation in everyday life.* Hyperion. (Original work published 1994)

Kabat-Zinn, J. (2013). *Full catastrophe living* (Rev. ed). Bantam Books.

Kerr, M. (2017). *One family's story: A primer on Bowen theory.* Georgetown Family Center, Inc.

Kessler, D. (2019). *Finding meaning: The sixth stage of grief.* Scribner.

Kübler-Ross, E. (1969). *On death and dying.* Macmillan.

Mellody, P. (2003). *Facing codependence: What it is, where it comes from, how it sabotages our lives.* Harper One. (Original work published 1989)

Miller, A. (1981). *The drama of the gifted child: The search for the true Self.* Basic Books, Inc.

Morrow, K. & Spencer, E. (2018). *CBT for anxiety: A step-by-step training manual for the treatment of fear, panic, worry and OCD.* PESI Publishing.

Nhất Hạnh, T. (1991). *Peace is every step: The path of mindfulness in everyday life.* Bantam Books.

Nhất Hạnh, T. (1999). *The miracle of mindfulness: An introduction to the practice of meditation.* Beacon Press.

Nhất Hạnh, T. (2011). *Peace is every breath.* HarperCollins.

Nhất Hạnh, T. Transforming feelings. *Living Life Fully.* https://livinglifefully.com/flo/flobetransformingfeelings.htm

Norwood, R. (2008). *Women who love too much* (Rev. ed.). Pocket Books.

Porges, S. (2011). *The polyvagal theory: Neurophysiological foundations of emotions, attachment, communication, and self-regulation.* W. W. Norton & Company.

Real, T. (2022). *What is RLT?* [Video]. Relational Life Institute. https://relationallife.com/level-1-training-what-is-rlt/?utm_source=ontraport&utm_medium=email&utm_campaign=level1email3

Schwartz, A. (2016). *The complex PTSD workbook: A mind-body approach to regaining emotional control and becoming whole.* Althea Press.

Schwartz, A. (2021). *The complex PTSD treatment manual: An integrative, mind-body approach to trauma recovery.* PESI Publishing.

Schwartz, R. C., & Sweezy, M. (2020). *Internal family systems therapy.* The Guilford Press.

Solomon, A. (2023). *Love every day: 365 relational self-awareness practices to help your relationship heal, grow, and thrive.* PESI Publishing.

Sweeton, J. (2019). *Trauma treatment toolbox: 165 brain-changing tips, tools & handouts to move therapy forward.* PESI Publishing.

Tawwab, N. G. (2023, March 16–19). *How boundaries can save your family relationships* [Conference presentation]. Psychotherapy Networker Symposium, Washington, DC, United States.

van der Kolk, B. (2014). *The body keeps the score: Brain, mind, and body in the healing of trauma.* Penguin Books.

Walker, P. (2013). *Complex PTSD: From surviving to thriving: A guide and map for recovering from childhood trauma.* Author.

Wegscheider-Cruse, S. (1989). *Another chance: Hope and health for the alcoholic family* (2nd ed.). Science & Behavior Books, Inc.

Wegscheider-Cruse, S., & Cruse, J. (2012). *Understanding codependency, updated & expanded: The science behind it & how to break the cycle.* Health Communications, Inc.

Whitfield, C. L. (1991). *Co-dependence: Healing the human condition: The new paradigm for helping professionals and people in recovery.* Health Communications, Inc.

Woititz, J. G. (1990). *Adult children of alcoholics, expanded edition.* Health Communications, Inc.

Yoder, B. (1990). *The recovery resource book.* Simon & Schuster, Inc.

Zelvin, E. (2004). Treating the partners of substance abusers. In S. L. A. Straussner (Ed.), *Clinical work with substance abusing clients* (pp. 264–283). The Guilford Press.

Acknowledgments

This book has its own backstory and path—as most books do—filled with people and experiences along the way for which I am grateful.

My gratitude path begins with my Al-Anon ancestors who pointed me in the direction of my first book of daily readings. As I began my own codependency recovery thirty-eight years ago, Al-Anon's daily readers gave me a foundational touchstone for the changes I wanted to make for me. Whether I was hearing the readings in meetings or reading them on my own, the wisdom of the people who wrote them and those who I spoke with about them made a world of difference in my ability to live with more serenity and appreciation for me.

Traveling along my gratitude path, I am grateful for the clinician who asked me at the end of one of my webinars to recommend a book of readings for people in recovery from codependency. I was speaking of the importance of intentional daily connection with our selves as we work on self-recovery. Their question inspired me to start writing this book of readings—weaving current knowledge and guidance with the foundations of my early recovery.

With a partial draft written and submitted as a book proposal, I was thrilled to receive a quick and enthusiastic book acceptance from the PESI Publishing team. Thank you, Kate Sample, Roseanne Cheng, Chelsea Thompson, G. Panzer, Abby Isackson, Alissa Schneider, and Jenny Miller for being such a great group of people to work with! Over and over, I appreciate your editorial talents, respectful attention to detail, and all that I learn from you about writing.

With the book acceptance in hand, I settled into writing it in my writer's studio at an arts center here in rural Virginia. Located on 100 wooded acres at the base of a mountain range, this haven for artists provides me with an amazing space to create and to be. Thank you, Karen and James, for my studio and for inspiring conversations scattered throughout our creative days.

And, I am grateful for the literal paths through the woods just outside my studio door. Most evenings at dusk, I walk into the woods. It is like a sanctuary for me—the tall trees, the silence, the rocky creek flowing off the mountains, birds in the sky, pine cones on the path, the seasonal changes. I am alone and love it. I settle into being—clearing my mind, relaxing my body, and feeling grateful beyond measure.

About the Author

Nancy L. Johnston, MS, LPC, LSATP, MAC, NCC, is a licensed professional counselor and licensed substance abuse treatment practitioner in private practice in Lexington, VA, US. With 48 years of clinical experience, Nancy is a master addiction counselor and an American Mental Health Counselors Association diplomate in substance abuse and co-occurring disorders.

She has authored three books on codependency: *Disentangle: When You've Lost Your Self in Someone Else* (2nd ed., 2020), *My Life as a Border Collie: Freedom from Codependency* (2012), and *The Clinician's Codependency Treatment Workbook: 66 Self-Recovery Strategies for Clients Who Lose Themselves in Others* (2024).

Nancy has digital seminars for clinicians on treating codependency produced with PESI, including "Codependence: Treatment Strategies for Clients Who Lose Themselves in Others," "The Codependency Treatment Guide: CBT, Somatic Strategies and More to Disentangle Clients from Dysfunctional Relationships and Recover Self," and "Advanced Codependency Treatment: A Complete Guide to CBT, Somatic, and Family of Origin Strategies to Disentangle Clients from Toxic Relationships and Recover Self."

Nancy offers online self-recovery workshops and delights in designing and facilitating Codependence Camp twice a year at a retreat site in Virginia, US. Codependence Camp has been in operation since 2004.

Over the past 25 years, Nancy has presented at numerous conferences, including the Cape Cod Symposium on Addictive Disorders, the Carolinas Conference for Addiction and Recovery, Addiction: Focus on Women, the Virginia Summer Institute for Addiction Studies, the American Mental Health Counselors Association's Annual Conference, the Virginia Counselors Association's Annual Conference, and specialty docket training for the Virginia Supreme Court. She has been a faculty member for the Psychotherapy Networker Symposium and the Ferentz Institute, and her work was included in a *New York Times* article on enmeshment in relationships.

Nancy loves her country home on a river in the Valley of Virginia. When she is not teaching or writing, she is enjoying extended time with family and friends, gardening, collaging, writing haiku, dancing, walking in the woods, and sitting by the river.

More information about Nancy and her work is available at her website: https://www.nancyljohnston.com.